Uniform with this volume:
These Spindrift Pages
On the Ivory Stages
Not for Ambition or Bread

THE STRUT AND
TRADE OF CHARMS

THE STRUT AND TRADE OF CHARMS

THEODORE DALRYMPLE

MIRABEAU PRESS

Published by Mirabeau Press

PO Box 4281

West Palm Beach, FL 33401

ISBN: 979-8-9939674-0-0

First Edition

MIRABEAU

I labour by singing light
Not for ambition or bread
Or the strut and trade of charms
On the ivory stages
But for the common wages
Of their most secret heart.
Not for the proud man apart
From the raging moon I write
On these spindrift pages...

In My Craft or Sullen Art, Dylan Thomas

This is the fourth volume of a series of little books whose only purpose has been to please myself in the hope of pleasing a few others, and perhaps to demonstrate that human life is so infinitely varied, inconsistent and unpredictable that no mere theory could explain it or catch it in the coarse mesh of its net. I have succeeded in giving pleasure to myself, but how far I have succeeded in pleasing others is not for me to judge.

In my possession is a curious little volume, dated 1880 and bound in vellum, of the title *Journals and Journalism: With a Guide for Literary Beginners*. It is by John Oldcastle, a pseudonym used by Wilfrid Meynell (1852–1948). Meynell was a Quaker turned Catholic, prolific as a journalist and as a father. Among his eight children were the novelist Viola Meynell and the founder of the Nonesuch Press, Francis Meynell, that specialised in useful anthologies of classic authors such as Donne, Swift and Hazlitt. Although forgotten now, Wilfrid Meynell moved in elevated literary circles, for among his friends and acquaintances were Robert Louis Stevenson, Thomas Hardy, W.B. Yeats and G.K. Chesterton, all of whom were regular visitors to his home.

Sir John Oldcastle, executed in 1417, was Shakespeare's model for Falstaff, and presumably Meynell chose the pseudonym for its Falstaffian resonance, though I can find no such resonance in *Journals and Journalism*. Meynell-Oldcastle was young himself when he wrote his tract, and his beginnings in the trade must have been fresh in his mind when he wrote it. One of the chapters is titled *Declined with Thanks* and is about rejection letters from editors, or what would now be rejection e-mails, if someone who sent an unsolicited contribution to a publication or publisher were now lucky enough to receive one. In the author's day, courtesy was probably more assiduously practised by editors than it is today, but I suppose one must take into account the enormous, probably exponential, increase in the number of scribblers since those more spacious times before condemning utterly the unmannerliness of our times. Of course, there are now untold opportunities for self-publication that did not exist in those

3

days, but in all likelihood not more than one in a hundred thousand of the self-published receives any kind of notice. Even today, people want a literary filter — a publisher, the editor of a journal — who will act as a guarantor against complete rubbish.

Therefore, the phenomenon of rejection is not a thing unknown even in times of self-publication, and Meynell-Oldcastle writes as if he knows whereof he speaks:

> No consolation that we can offer here will be able to mitigate the sting of a first — or indeed, of a second or a third — reception of this courteous but inexorable form of refusal. It is not until after one or two acceptances of MS [manuscripts], that a rejection becomes in any degree tolerable. When the acceptances outnumber the rejections, indeed, 'Declined with thanks' will generally cease to cause a serious pang.

This, I confess, has not been altogether my experience. Since the publication of my first article in 1983, I must have published something between five and ten thousand articles, but still the occasional rejection comes as a stab in the heart. No doubt this is the manifestation of a fragile ego.

Meynell-Oldcastle describes at some length the various reasons given for refusal or rejection, some of which give spurious hope to the writer and some of which are so patently ridiculous that they anger the recipient. A favourite among publishers rejecting a manuscript (or PDF) is that the proposed book does not fit their list, as if their list were itself a work of art, carefully sculpted or structured.

4

The rejected author has to react to his rejection constrictively, but this is very difficult, for it requires nice judgment, which most of us do not have. Some rejections might be in the long-term interests of the writer, to preserve him from later embarrassment. My first book was rejected (though once very nearly accepted), and now I am glad of it, though at the time, of course, I attributed the rejection to the ill-judgment of the publishers. Meynell-Oldcastle gives examples of famous authors and now famous books that met with rejections, among them *Robinson Crusoe*, repeatedly rejected though it made a fortune for its eventual publisher.[1] Success rarely comes at the first effort: but then, success rarely comes at all. It does not follow from the fact that *Robinson Crusoe* was rejected and became a perennial best-seller that any rejected book will one day be a perennial best-seller.

Success is to aspiring authors what the jackpot is to the habitual users of the fruit machines in Las Vegas. In Las Vegas it is a matter of luck, and perhaps persistence, but in literature it is a matter of talent of some sort. Every writer believes that he has it, and while it might be true that no book is undeservedly remembered, it is also true that many a deserving book is forgotten. This asymmetry keeps alive the hopes, often delusive, of at least critical, if not financial, success, and confronts the rejected author with the difficulty of assessing the reason for his own failure. Is it because what he has written is of no worth, or because the world, in the form of editors, critics, readers, and so forth, has obstinately,

---

[1] A story repeated a quarter of a millennium later by the first *Harry Potter* book and its publisher, Bloomsbury.

ignorantly and even dishonestly refused to recognise its high quality, originality and other virtues?

The aspiring author must be modest enough to consider the defects of his work but self-confident enough to believe that, if not immediately, he will at least one day say something that will be heard. This is a difficult path to tread without veering off into madness. Strait is the gate, and narrow is the path, that leads to correct self-evaluation.

But correct self-evaluation can also be the enemy of achievement, not only in writing but in all endeavours. Not all endeavours might be equal in intrinsic value (though a scale of values is difficult to justify beyond all doubt and possible criticism), but success in any of them will require obstinate self-belief, which will more often than not be unjustified. The road to excellence is paved with mediocrity.

How things have changed, in some respects, since Meynell-Oldcastle's time! He gives advice to the beginners of 1880. Do not, he says, send manuscripts with embossed coats-of-arms or coronets, for this would imply that the author does not really need to be published, at least not for the sake of money (he does not mention that it will provoke envy or inverted snobbery in editors). Write on white paper not blue, says Meynell-Oldcastle, and use black ink: this will assist the compositors, who are now not so much a dying as an extinct breed.

Compositors still existed, however, when I started on my glorious literary career. I sent in my manuscripts by post or dictated them down the telephone to copy-takers, valiant women typists who typed everything with an admirable, value-free sang-froid, like that of a doctor listening to the confessions of his patients.

How quaint the past soon seems to us in an age of technology!

Much has been written about the uselessness of erudition, which after all dies with its possessor, but less, perhaps, about uselessness in general. In the introduction to his book, *Le Studio de l'inutilité,* The Studio of Uselessness, Simon Leys, one of the greatest essayists who has lived in my lifetime, says, 'I hope to remain true to the teachings of the Studio of Uselessness [an informal little academy for refugee Chinese scholars in Singapore in which Leys studied when he was young]... at least in the obvious sense given to the name by Zhuang Zi.'

Leys quotes the latter as follows: 'All people understand the use of what is useful, but they do not know the use of the useless,' to which Leys adds, 'After all, this sort of uselessness is the foundation even of the essential values of our common humanity.'

This must be true, because there have to be ends in themselves that require no further justification for there to be anything useful at all: for if there were no such ends, we should have an endless regress of ends, so there could be no grounds for preferring one thing or course of action to another.

Pedantry is a kind of perverted erudition, and it has its own delights, not least of which is that it is an end in itself. Pedantry keeps other thoughts at bay and does not ask itself what it is for any more than does stamp-collecting. It is a kind of displacement activity, of the kind that a mouse indulges in when cornered by a cat, washing its paws to disguise its terror from itself. Pedantry is a defence against, or the staving off of, the Second Law of Thermodynamics, according to which chaos will always win in the end.

Pedantry and bibliomania are closely associated. I don't think that I am truly a bibliomane, at least not in the sense of the Reverend Thomas Frognall Dibdin's famous book, *Bibliomania; or Book Madness*, first published in 1809. It is true that I now live in and through books to an extraordinary extent, quite outside the statistical range of normal. After an hour or two of not reading, I long to return to the printed page. It is also true that I find it hard not to enter a bookshop if there is one nearby, especially should it be of second-hand books. Moreover, I like and am excited by rarities, even rarities that are rare precisely because no one wants them. It is true also that I prefer a handsome or early edition to any other, especially if it happens to have been signed or dedicated by the author, or has previously belonged to someone of note, but it is not rational to value a book for anything but its contents. Yet, as I have indicated, I am not really a bibliomaniac in Dibdin's sense or a victim of what he ironically calls 'this fatal disease.'

Dibdin (1776–1847) adopted the definition of bibliomania in Etienne Gabriel Peignot's book, *Dictionnaire raisonné de bibliologie* (which Dibdin, being notorious for his combination of pedantry and inaccuracy, shortened to *Dictionnaire de bibliologie*):

[He, Peignot] defines the Bibliomania to be a passion for possessing books, not so much to be instructed by them, as to gratify the eye by looking at them. He who is affected by this mania knows books only by their titles and dates, and is rather seduced by the exterior than the interior.

Dibdin goes on to list eight symptoms of bibliomania: the passion for large paper copies, for uncut copies, illustrated copies, unique copies, vellum copies, first editions, true editions and black letter [English Gothic] editions.

A pedant, of course, would demand an operational definition of what constitutes 'a passion': a simple preference would hardly be enough. For example, I have often bought a first edition of a novel in preference to a second or third, and will even have paid more for it, but I would not go a hundred miles or bankrupt myself to obtain it. As Dibdin points out, this desire for first editions is not strictly rational, or rational at all, insofar as 'they are in many respects superfluous... [because] the labour of subsequent editors[2] has corrected their errors, and superseded by a great fund of additional matter, the necessity of consulting them.' This applies not only to works of learning but to those of literature. Coleridge reworked *The Rime of the Ancient Mariner* for many years, and no one but a literary scholar would be interested in the first version: though it must be admitted that, in the case of De Quincey's *Confessions of an English Opium Eater*, the first edition is much superior in literary quality to the greatly expanded second.

Passion in Dibdin's sense means a desire that is inordinate,

---

[2] To say nothing of that of the authors themselves.

though what is inordinate is, perhaps, not itself definable.

Dibdin refers to the passion for outsized copies and here again I fail to meet a criterion for the diagnosis of the disease. I have two copies of books that might be regarded as outsized, being very large by comparison with their content, and which one could not easily take to bed with one. The first is a copy of Thomas Gray's *Poems*, and the second (in three volumes) Ruskin's *Praeterita*. I bought them not because I longed for them or had searched for them, but because, as the climber of Mount Everest might have said, they were there.[3]

Dibdin says that 'this symptom [together with that of specially printed editions] of the Bibliomania is at the present day, both general and violent:' and to this day, French publishers are inclined to offer specially printed copies of new works in limited editions sold at inflated prices.

Dibdin remarks on the passion for uncut copies, which also persists and is indeed strange, since it precludes any inspection of the book's contents. 'This is probably the most extraordinary of the symptoms of the Bibliomania,' says Dibdin. 'It may be defined as a passion to possess books of which the edges [of the pages] have never been sheared by the binder's tools.'

But what more can you rationally want of a book than that it should be well-printed and well-bound? Yet the word 'uncut' is still one of praise in booksellers' catalogues; but I confess that when I come across a book with uncut pages, I invariably cut it, no doubt reducing its value thereby.

---

[3] George Mallory (1886–1924), who died in his attempt on Everest, is reputed to have replied 'Because it is there' when asked why he wanted to climb Everest.

The first edition of Dibdin's book was only 81 pages long, the text being far shorter than the footnotes, the author's implicit satire on pedantry. I could not possibly afford a first edition, and therefore my edition is a twenty-first century reprint, edited by Peter Danckwerts. The latter's endnotes to the text and its footnotes are even more voluminous than both together, being one page the longer. The endnotes to the footnotes to the text explain to the modern reader who were the many persons mentioned by Dibdin in the text and footnotes, and the sources, and in some cases the translations, of Dibdin's quotations.

The length of the endnotes was surely another satire on pedantry: and how I should have loved to join in the game! I would have liked to add footnotes to the endnotes to the footnotes, to satisfy my own thirst for pedantry. For example, to the endnote on William Lisle Bowles (1762–1850), I would have liked to add that his poems exerted a profound influence on Coleridge, who reverenced his sonnets which are now completely forgotten. And to the endnote of Richard Mead, the English physician, I would have liked to append that he wrote the first book on poisons in English.

Of the making of many books there is no end, says Ecclesiastes, and much study is a weariness of the flesh: to which I would like to add a footnote, that to the appending of footnotes there is no end, and much pedantry is a delight of the unimaginative.

Molly Lefebure must have been a remarkable person. For five

years she was secretary to Keith Simpson, who became the most famous forensic pathologist in Britain, in the days when murders were infrequent enough to be known by a sobriquet and when both pathologists and defence counsel were national celebrities, albeit in a manner relatively modest by comparison with celebrity today. Molly Lefebure was Simpson's secretary during the war years, and in his autobiography, *Forty Years of Murder*, Simpson recounts how, during an air-raid, he once took shelter with her under a post-mortem table in the mortuary of Guy's Hospital.

Whenever he was called out to examine a putrefying body found in a field or copse, he took her with him to record his observations. She must have been a person of more than usual fortitude to have stuck it out, the more so as she was a person of refined taste and background. She wrote a memoir of her experiences in those war years but then, after her marriage, went to live in the Lake District, where she became a respected scholar of the Lake Poets and English Romanticism. Two such disparate careers speak to considerable resources of intellect and character.

In pursuit of a literary project of mine, I read a biography by her of Samuel Taylor Coleridge up to the year 1816, titled *Samuel Taylor Coleridge: A Bondage of Opium*. I was attracted to this long and heavy book not only by its relevance to my project, as yet hardly started, but by the photograph of the author on the book's back cover. She is in the country, wearing the kind of sweater suitable neither for very cold nor for hot weather. On her face is a faint and unposed smile, that of a person who neither seeks nor eschews publicity. Her hair is quite but not very closely cropped — one might say it was *sensible*, considering the windiness of the region. It is a feminine style, but suitable to a woman who spends much time out of doors.

What most attracted me to the picture, however, was that she held a Yorkshire terrier in precisely the way that we used to hold our own beloved Yorkshire terrier, Ramses, tucked under her arm. He is seen in profile, with his ears pricked, looking out at the world with the same passionate intensity that Ramses had, as if nothing in the world were uninteresting to him. As I write this, it is nearly seventeen years since Ramses died, longer than we had him with us, but it is no cliché to say that he lives still in our hearts. When I showed this picture of Molly Lefebure to my wife, no words were necessary.[4]

I am not at one, however, with the author in her attitude to Coleridge's addiction to laudanum (tincture of opium in alcohol), much as I admire her industry and scholarship. Nor do I entirely share her admiration for the subject of her biography, towards whom I must control my antipathy. I cannot even think of him as having been among the greatest of English poets, let alone as a great man. He possessed great ability, of course, and must have had enormous charisma, for he attracted men of the quality of William Wordsworth, Charles Lamb, Josiah Wedgwood, Sir Humphrey Davy and William Hazlitt. He is said to have been a wonderful conversationalist, though I suspect he was more of a monologuist. He was often a parasite, a liar, a deceiver, an

---

[4] Ramses was a companion in whose company we were never lonely, never sad and never bored.

unscrupulous plagiarist and a terminal self-dramatiser, so much so that I have difficulty in believing in the sincerity of almost anything that he wrote. His use of the exclamation mark exceeded by far that of any other author known to me; he was, in a way, a very modern person, inasmuch as he valued strong emotions, or the expression of strong emotions (which is not quite the same thing), for their own sake. I think there is something fraudulent about him, and his inability to finish either *Christabel* or *Kubla Khan* was typical of the man. It was characteristic that he lied shamelessly about the reasons for his inability to finish the latter, the real reason being inability to do so. It is true, however, that *In Xanadu* has wonderful lines, albeit of uncertain meaning:

> Weave a circle round him thrice
> And close your eyes with holy dread,
> For he on honey-dew hath fed
> And drunk the milk of Paradise.

But a relatively few lines of exceptional beauty do not (for me) make him one of the glories of our literature.

I have a little book of Coleridge's poems which I have had since I was about ten, bound in a dark green cloth that hints at leather, and a small part of whose front cover has been slightly nibbled at by mice. It has an introduction by Sir Henry Newbolt, the forgotten poet whose most famous line, 'Play up! play up! and play the game!' adorns, or used to adorn, a wall of Lord's cricket ground. The poem and this line made a great impression on me, insofar as they suggested that a victory achieved by cheating was no victory at all.

In his introduction, Newbolt (who died in 1938) takes what was then the conventional view, that romanticism such as that of Coleridge liberated English poetry from what he, Newbolt, called 'the frigid and abstract style of eighteenth-century verse,' a century of 'conventionality, materialism and safety-first.'

It is true, of course, that poets could not go on writing in alexandrines for ever, and that much eighteenth century verse must seem bloodless to us now: but it must also be remembered that most verse or poetry of any age will seem defective or uninteresting to its successor, if only because most poets are not great. All I can say is that for me, Gray's *Elegy* is far superior, with more genuine feeling, than anything that Coleridge ever wrote, or at least what of his that I have read. Gray's thought and feeling is not original, but it is not the role or purpose of poetry to extend original thought. The Romantic cult of sincerity and authenticity resulted in precisely the opposite (at least, in many cases). Compare the following lines of Coleridge with those of Gray:

> Ye Clouds! that far above me float and pause
> Whose pathless march no mortal may control!
> Ye Ocean-Waves! that whereso'er ye roll,
> Yield homage only to eternal laws!

Coleridge apostrophises the woods (Ye Woods!); there are five exclamation marks in eight lines. This is emotional exhaustion by means of punctuation.

Now for Gray, as he writes of the poor who have been interred in the country churchyard:

Let not Ambition mock their useful toil,
Their homely joys and destinies obscure;
Nor Grandeur hear with a disdainful smile
The short and simple annals of the poor.

The boasts of heraldry, the pomp of pow'r,
And all that beauty, all that wealth e'er gave
Awaits alike th'inevitable hour;
The paths of glory lead but to the grave.

This is finer and expressive of deeper feeling than anything
Coleridge ever wrote.[5] And so is Doctor Johnson's touching
epitaph to Robert Levet, the humble surgeon whom Johnson
befriended and lodged in his house (surgeons in those days
could be humble). No exclamation marks are necessary for the
reader to understand the depth of Johnson's feeling:

Condemn'd to Hope's delusive mine,
As on we tread from day to day.
By sudden blasts, or slow decline,
Our social comforts drop away.

Well tried through many a varying year,
See Levet to the grave descend:

---

[5] Though not Keats. In *Frost at Midnight*, Coleridge came near to
sincerity. The lines from Gray that I have quoted express my own
sentiments whenever I walk in a churchyard or cemetery.

Officious[6], innocent, sincere,
Of every friendless name the friend.

Depth of feeling is not proportional to extravagance of expression.

In my little collection (or accumulation) of literary curiosities is a tiny book titled *Confessions of an English Hachish-Eater*. Like the much more famous *Confessions of an English Opium-Eater*, it was published anonymously, but unlike the latter, it had not been attributed to any author beyond reasonable doubt. It is generally thought, however, to be the work of William Laird Clowes (1856–1905), a journalist and naval historian who in 1902 was knighted for his work.

Published in 1884, it is said to be exceedingly rare (I begin to sound like a bookseller's catalogue), and few are the public collections with a copy. How and when I came by it, I cannot now remember; but my copy once belonged to the Reverend William Kyle Westwood Chafy-Chafy who lived at Rous Lench Court in Worcestershire. He bought the book of W. & H. Smith, booksellers in Evesham, also in Worcestershire. These two Smiths were the founders of the still-extant *Evesham Journal* and are not to be confused with the W.H. Smith, also a bookseller and newsagent, who founded the giant retail chain that sells stationery, rubbers, pencils, labels, marker

---

[6] Officious here means performing of his office, curing where he could, bringing comfort where he could not, as Doctor Johnson remarks.

pens, magazines, and best-selling books, all displayed with maximum unattractiveness.

As to the Reverend William Kyle Westwood Chafy-Chafy (it seems almost an act of *lèse-majesté* to shorten his name, as it was to shorten that of His Excellency the Life-President, Ngwazi Dr H. Kamuzu Banda[7]), he lived from 1841 to 1916. I have been unable, at least with the effort that I am prepared to devote to it, to find out much about him. According to *Wikidata*, he was a human and a male, which did not much surprise me, and his main achievement, as far as any trace left on the internet is concerned, is his remarkable bookplate, which is round and with an armorial decoration. Rous Lench Court, in which he lived, is a very large, half-timbered, mainly Victorian house, grand but aesthetically something of a mess, now used for wedding receptions. Perhaps the Reverend William Kyle Westwood Chafy-Chafy was open-minded, or perhaps the subject of the book did not carry the emotional charge that it does today.

The author, whoever he was, begins his short book by remarking on how difficult it was in England to come by good quality hashish, not a complaint much heard today. Certainly, supply seems greatly to have improved since then; but at the time, locally grown hemp, says the author (quite correctly), contained little of the active ingredient. Moreover, imported hemp had often deteriorated by the time it arrived.

Knowing this, I took some pains to assure myself that the

---

[7] First President of Malawi, formerly Nyasaland, President for Life until he was overthrown.

dried hemp from which I prepared my hachish came from India and was of recent growth. Having procured the raw material, I carefully picked out the flowering tops of a number of fine plants and macerated them in spirit, pressing out, distilling and evaporating the result to the consistency of birdlime.

He goes on to say that English doctors are willing to admit that they know very little about the drug, though *extractum Cannabis indicae* is present in the British pharmacopoeia and was used in small doses for treating certain diseases of women, rheumatism and one or two other maladies. Of its psychotropic properties, they knew nothing.

The author then describes the effects of his product (later, he recommends the use of hashish-containing Turkish delight to avoid the bitterness of its taste, the oral route being the only one he knows). He said that he was cautious and took an amount that he increased day by day. At the lowest doses, it had no effect at all, but:

Late one afternoon... I swallowed six grains dissolved in a spoonful of brandy... Half an hour later I dined, forgoing my usual cup of coffee. I settled myself into a comfortable armchair and lighted a cigar. I was not drowsy, but felt lazy and disinclined to move, and this tendency was speedily increased by an agreeable sensation of warmth that pervaded the body... My feet and hands successively "went to sleep" for a few moments, and when they woke again, they tingled as if they had been frost-bitten, and were rapidly regaining their natural condition. The frequent recurrence of these sensations concentrated my attention upon myself; and little by little I fell into complete silence and then lay back in my chair. Although I did not lose consciousness for more than three or four seconds at a time, consecutive thought now became irksome if not impossible; and I voluntarily surrendered myself to the dreaminess that came over me.

I suppose there are people who like this fuzziness of mind: all I can say is that I do not (except a little when waking from sleep). Passing through towns in England, I can divide them into two classes or categories: those so boring that young people crave for stimulants, and those so horrible and degraded that young people seek calmants, that is to say a choice between artificial excitement and artificial tranquillity, with the effort of thought suppressed in both cases.

Taking bigger doses still of hashish, the author experiences dreams of hallucinatory intensity and describes them, in my opinion with a great deal more coherence than they could have had in the original, and therefore with more than a little editorial alteration. But one experience seems to me very well described, after he had taken hashish at a friend's house after dinner:

It was a summer evening, and the sun had just set as I shook hands with my host at his door, and descended the steps. No sooner did I reach the pavement than I suddenly lost my normal consciousness, and was apparently liberated from the normal shackles of the body. In a moment I was passing through the warm air at a height varying from between four and ten feet from the earth: and around and below me people were staring at my strange performance. I paid no heed to them, however, unless, indeed, I scornfully regarded them as lesser beings. To me my method of progress did not seem to be in the slightest abnormal. I skated rather than walked, and moved without any effort; and I have a vivid recollection of all my sensations.

After various other psychic adventures, including pursuit by a host of little elf-like creatures, which he found most amusing, he arrived home:

I was in my own room and in bed. The lamp on my table was lighted; and I afterwards discovered that I had not only lighted it but also trimmed its wick. Since my return I had spoken to members of my family, and they had noticed nothing amiss with me.

At the end of the book, the author draws his conclusions from his experiences, which he regards as positive, give or take a nightmare or two. He has an imaginary conversation with someone he calls Dr Omnibus, that is to say the average man on the Clapham omnibus beloved of British lawyers, with all his common sense and prejudices, including medical ones:

"But it will certainly weaken your brain," says that benevolent gentleman, Dr. Omnibus.
Dr. Omnibus, with all my respects, is a fool. It is he who

says, "Don't drink beer—it's adulterated. Don't drink spirits—they destroy the coat of the stomach. Don't drink tea or coffee—it ruins the digestion and deadens the nerves. And, above all, don't drink water—it is poisonous."

You, reader, and I have heard him say all this; and in similar strains, he makes onslaughts on tobacco, on corsets, on lobster salads, and on a great many other good things. Do you heed him? Of course not. Neither do I. But we all know that the old gentleman must have something to prattle about.

Dr. Omnibus is not always such a complete fool, however; and the argument between him and the author is not entirely settled to this day, 140 years later, and perhaps never will be.[8]

A slight illness recently laid me low, that is to say sufficiently weak that I had to go to bed, but without great suffering. I swiftly realised the advantages of being indisposed in this way: I was excused for a time all the boring tasks of normal daily existence that everyone who does not have a host of attendants must perform. For once I could do absolutely nothing with a good conscience, indeed I was enjoined to do nothing, any attempt at activity of any kind being interpreted not as helpfulness but as a kind of stubbornness, almost a wilful effort

---

[8] Is it worth pointing out that William Laird Clowes, if indeed he was the author, was a self-confessed habitual smoker and died at the comparatively early age of 49?

to make myself worse.

The illness, as I have said, was slight; and after a few days my body began to get the better of whatever virus had invaded it. I could tell that it had not caused a very severe illness — more of an indisposition, really — because I was not altogether pleased to get better (very different was it when, as a young man, I underwent the crisis of a viral pneumonia, a sweating attack after which, though weak and wrung out, I knew that I was cured once and for all, and was very glad of it). As I improved from this indisposition, I would have to rejoin everyday life, with all its disagreeable and frankly boring obligations. It is one thing to be bored without having to make an effort, and another to have to make an effort and still be bored. I could quite understand those increasingly many who extend both the duration and severity of their symptoms by means of subterfuge. I was a little tempted to do so myself, to prolong the period when I was waited on hand and foot: and, after all, there was little chance, provided I took a few precautions, of being exposed as a fraud. It is not easy always to distinguish what a person cannot from what he will not do, and if one plays at incapacity long enough, incapacitated is what one becomes.

The advantages of invalidism, at least for a time, are succinctly described (from personal acquaintance) by Charles Lamb[9], in his essay, *The Convalescent*. It is to be found in the *Last Essays of Elia*, though in his case the illness was more severe, as illnesses tended to be in the late eighteenth and early nineteenth century, when a mere scratch might result in fatal

---

[9] Charles Lamb 1775–1834, Mary Lamb 1764–1847

septicaemia. Lamb was ill of 'a pretty severe fit of indisposition… under the name of a nervous fever'—a diagnosis which conveys little meaning to a modern doctor. No doubt our own diagnostic categories would convey little meaning to an eighteenth century doctor, but I have sufficient faith in scientific progress to assert, even if philosophical relativists would find it arrogant, that we are superior to our eighteenth-century confreres in the matter of nosological accuracy.

At any rate, Lamb's illness 'reduced [him] to an incapacity of reflecting on any topic foreign to itself.' This one sentence brought to my mind a painful memory, associated with a feeling of guilt. As a student, I had a friend, a girl of the sweetest character, saintly would hardly be too strong a word, a student of languages, who one day described to us — medical students — some faint symptoms that we diagnosed, alas correctly, as those of multiple sclerosis. I lost contact with her for several decades, and tried to resume it, by which time, after valiantly battling to remain a teacher for as long as possible, she was bedridden. When at last I spoke to her by telephone, her speech was affected, and all her talk, as was natural, was of her condition. Alas, she died soon thereafter, before I had time to visit her (hence the guilt). I should have gone immediately, without delay, but as the Romanian peasant saying has it, the whole village is on fire, but grandmother wants to finish combing her hair.

It was not her fault that she spoke only of her condition, for what else could she have spoken of, having been bedridden for several years? Lamb says:

How sickness enlarges the dimensions of a man's self to himself! He is his own exclusive object. Supreme selfishness is inculcated upon him as his only duty... He has nothing to think of but how to get well.[10] What passes out of doors, or within them, so he hears not the jarring of them, affects him not.

There is a good lesson for every doctor in Lamb's essay, which every medical student ought to read: namely that the doctor is more important to the patient than the patient can ever be to him.

To the world's business he [the patient] is dead. He understands not what the occupations of mortals are; only he has a glimmering conceit of some such thing, when the doctor makes his daily call;[11] and even in the lines of that busy face, he reads no multiplicity of patients, but solely conceives of himself as *the sick man.* To what other uneasy couch the good man is hastening, when he slips out of his chamber... is no speculation which he can at present entertain. He thinks only of the regular return of the same phenomenon at the same hour to-morrow.

The ill person is a monarch in or of his household, around whom everything revolves. To become convalescent is to lose

---

[10] In my friend's case, she had nothing to think of but her own inevitable deterioration. Note, incidentally, Lamb's appropriate use of the exclamation mark by comparison with the use to which it (rarely singly) was put by his friend, Samuel Taylor Coleridge.
[11] Whether at home or on his hospital rounds.

this sovereignty. The very doctor changes his attitude towards him and talks to him of the world almost as in a social encounter. The silence around him disappears, the looks of solicitude also. Lamb calls convalescence 'the flat swamp left by the ebb of sickness, yet far enough from the terra firma of established health.' While during his convalescence Lamb's editor demands an article from him, Lamb remarks:

> … from the giant of self-importance, which I was so lately, you have me once more again in my natural pretensions — the lean and meagre figure of your essayist.

I don't suppose many people read the once classic *Essays of Elia* and *Last Essays*, the very genre itself of essay (if not of reading altogether) being unfashionable. But Lamb was a very interesting man, with a tragic life that he met with superficial gaiety—by which I mean not that he was a superficial man but that his gaiety was a veneer over his suffering and melancholy. His sister, eleven years older than he, with whom he lived during her periods of sanity, killed their mother during one of her bouts of madness—which grew longer and more frequent with age. This was the event that clouded their lives for ever.

Mary Lamb was probably treated, at least in certain respects, more humanely than she would now have been. At every reappearance of her madness, she was sent to a private madhouse where she may, or may not, have been treated with kindness or treated with cruelty. Between times, she was allowed home and was the principal author of the Lambs' most famous book, *Tales from Shakespeare* (that I read as a child).

In an admirable letter to Coleridge, written shortly after Mary had stabbed their mother to death, Lamb wrote:

> Within a day or 2 after the fatal ONE, we drest for dinner a tongue, which we had salted for some weeks in the house.[12] As I sat down a feeling of REMORSE struck me,—this tongue poor Mary got for ME, & can I now partake of it NOW, when she is far AWAY[13]—a thought occur'd and relieved me,—if I give into this way of feeling, there is not a chair, a room, an object in our rooms, that will not awaken the keenest griefs. I must arise above such weaknesses—I hope this was not want of true feeling. I did not let this tho' carry me too far. On the very 2d day (I date from the day of HORRORS) as is usual in such cases there were a matter of 20 people I do think supping on our ROOM -. They prevailed on me to eat *with them* (for to eat I never refused) they were all making merry! In my Room—some had come from friendship, some from busy curiosity, & some from INTEREST; I was going to partake with THEM, when my recollection came that my poor dead mother was lying in the next room, the very next room, a mother who thro' life wished nothing but her children's welfare—indignation, the rage of grief, something like remorse, rushed upon my mind in an agony of emotion,—I found

---

[12] Tongue was one of my favourite dishes as a child. You rarely see it now — like blackcurrants or gooseberries, two other favourites of mine.

[13] In the madhouse.

my way mechanically to the adjoining room, and fell on my knees by the SIDE of her coffin, asking forgiveness of heaven, & sometimes of her, for forgetting her SO SOON. Tranquillity returned, & it was the only violent emotion that master'd me, & I think it did me good.

Imagining oneself in his situation — he returned one evening to find his mad sister wielding the bloody knife with which she had stabbed their mother through the heart (perhaps more than once) and with which she had also stabbed their dementing father, who was injured — one cannot remain unmoved by this dignified epistle.

Having had more to do professionally with murders and murderers than perhaps the average citizen, though not as much as some, it is only natural that I should retain an interest in the subject: not that other people lack interest in it, to judge by the sales of books, fictional and non-fictional, concerning murder. Literature in general is full of it, though even in the worst of places murder, outside of war, is a comparatively rare event. But try to imagine *Crime and Punishment* without murder: what would be left? It is an interesting question as to why murder should so fascinate us; Freud said (though he was almost certainly mistaken) that dreams expressed wish-fulfilment, though wishes diverted by psychic mechanisms from their true object. Are crime novels to be explained in the same way? I do not see how we could go about proving such a theory. Has everyone someone (that is so say at least one person) whom he wishes dead and desires to kill?

I mentioned Molly Lefebure earlier, the redoubtable scholar of English Romantic poets who had been for five years secretary to Dr (later Professor) Keith Simpson, a well-brought up woman who accompanied him to the sites of gruesome murders, where rotting corpses had just been found. Simpson was for long one of the most eminent forensic pathologists in England, and in 1978 he published a best-selling memoir, *Forty Years of Murder*, of which my paperback edition is the thirteenth printing. On its cover it has the following encomia: 'One of the most absorbing volumes on murder I have ever read,' 'Fascinating and gripping,' and 'Gruesome indeed, but fascinating too.'

Near its beginning, where Simpson explains why he entered the field, there is a wonderful anecdote. Simpson was preparing to perform a post-mortem on an old man at the behest of the coroner, presumably because the old man's death was unexplained by previous illness. The body was lying on the slab, and before Simpson set to work, he asked the coroner's officer for information about the deceased, such as the nature of his work, that might be relevant to whatever he found.

> 'Well, sir,' said the coroner's officer, 'the man was an actor...'
> Before he could get any further, the mortuary attendant interjected:
> 'Gor blimey, if he's acting now, he's bloody good!'

This is the kind of gallows humour that I so appreciated in my time as a doctor in prison. I suspect, though I do not know, that such humour is now frowned upon officially, even forbidden, by simple-minded puritans, who take all speech in its most literal meaning. As to the expression *Gor blimey!*, it was still current when I was a boy, but I do not think it is much used now. A compression and mispronunciation of *God blind me!*, it always had an element of irony in it, and irony is not a feature of our age.

The scene in the mortuary took me back to the days when I attended, not with great enthusiasm, the post-mortems of patients in the hospital in which I worked and who had come under my care. My lack of enthusiasm was not, I am sorry to say, a manifestation of my sorrow for the departed, but of distaste for the procedure, the sound of the circular saw opening the chest being the least of it.

The first time I went to the hospital mortuary, there were two men standing in white rubber boots, one of them with a white rubber apron. He looked very distinguished, with a fine head of golden hair now going grey; the other looked a thorough degenerate, as if crushed by a hangover from the night before. I assumed that the former was the pathologist and the latter the mortuary assistant, but in fact it was the other way round. However, it was the attendant who performed all the post-mortems, having picked up the skills necessary to do so over the years. The pathologist, I was later told, was either drunk or hung over, without ever passing through a phase of sobriety, and was suspected also to have been a morphine addict. He was only present *pro forma*, to sign whatever the mortuary assistant wrote in reports as if the findings were his own.

Pathologists, however, are generally the most learned of all physicians. An old saw has it that a physician (or internist, in America), knows a lot but does nothing; a surgeon knows nothing but does a lot; and a pathologist knows everything but too late. This is all very far from the case; but sixty years ago, there was still something in it.

In general, I was in awe of pathologists' erudition, even if at times it seemed to veer off into pedantry.

Simpson was not only learned but contributed new learning. He had formidable powers of deduction from the smallest clues that would have escaped eyes and brains less sharp than his. He also had the necessary capacity for taking pains. If the stories he tells are dramatic, it is because they are the distillation of infinite labour, not only of his, but of the police detectives and specialist forensic scientists who were expert in very tiny fields of study, such as the splashing of blood on walls or the identity of hair. It takes a special kind of mind to become such an expert, and it is as well for us all that there are such minds.

Simpson practised in another era, in some respects better than our own, though of course less technically advanced. The police in his day did not see themselves as social workers with handcuffs and powers of arrest, and had an *esprit de corps*; and while there was, as with any large body of men, corruption among them, they were generally respected rather than being the object of contempt, as they are now.

There was, for example, the remarkable figure of Detective Chief Superintendent Walter Jones, of the Hampshire Criminal Investigation Department. Not long before his retirement, he had solved all thirty-nine murders that had been committed on his patch but was now faced by one that threatened to spoil his record. A Southampton taxi driver had been brutally beaten to death in his cab, and the only clue was a single fingerprint on the man's savings book (such documents existed then, I remember them because I had one), which had been used to draw out a small sum of money. The fingerprint corresponded to none known to the police: the culprit was a man without a criminal record. From this, Jones concluded that he must be young, and that furthermore a man who committed such a crime (half the human race, the female, could be ruled out *a priori*) would not commit only one crime, and he therefore ordered that all fingerprints taken subsequent to the crime should be compared with the one on the savings book. Sure enough, a young man called Stoneley was caught as he tried to break into a garage. Walter Jones retired after his fortieth triumph, his record intact, and went on in his retirement to run a pub in Hampshire which Simpson (who had performed the post-mortem on the taxi driver) patronised whenever he was in the vicinity. As my wife put it, 'It was a different world.'[14]

The story has interesting twists at the end. In his confession to the police, Stoneley tried to blame the victim for his own death, for not having sought medical assistance after Stoneley had attacked him. The fact that he must have been unconscious because his skull was stoved in and he was beyond medical assistance did not occur to him. This is powerful testimony to human powers of self-delusion.

---

[14] Walter Jones was the first person to be awarded the *Sherlock Holmes Pipe Prize* of the British Crime Writers' Association.

The second twist is that, five months after he had had his death sentence commuted to life imprisonment, he was married to a nineteen-year-old young woman called Pat Mundell. How odd human beings are! In my experience, few notorious murderers — especially of women — lack for declarations of love thereafter by women previously unknown to them. I haven't the space to go further into this strange phenomenon, nor would I have any explanation even if I had the space.

As I like acidity in fruit (sweetness repels me), so I like acerbity in writing and conversation. It dissolves verbiage; it encourages both concision and precision. No doubt (since every virtue is a vice if carried too far) it can end in pettifoggery, with such concern over the meaning of terms that nothing about the world can be said. I am reminded of Karl Popper's famous remark about Wittgenstein, that he spent so much time polishing his glasses that he never looked through them.

Of all novelists known to me — which is not an immense number — the most acerbic is undoubtedly Ivy Compton-Burnett, who died as little time ago as 1964, but over whom there lingers the faint odour of patchouli and mothballs. She lived most of her adult life as companion to two women in succession: in those days, people were sophisticated enough not only not to ask about the nature of their companionship, but not even to let the question enter their minds, as being none of their business.

Her novel, *Manservant and Maidservant*, was published in 1947. It must have been published early in that year, for it is inscribed by the purchaser *Cambridge, February 1947*. The inscription is in a cultivated hand in black ink, but cultivation in handwriting is not the same as legibility, and I had difficulty in deciphering the name. Olave Snitter? That sounded unlikely. Eventually, with the aid of a magnifying glass, I settled on Marie Soutter. Once I had done so, I could not read it in any other way, which demonstrates perhaps the power of preconception once it is established.

Marie Soutter: perhaps she was someone famous but unknown to me. Surely she could not have been the Marie Soutter who was 'the executive-assistant for two C-suite executives at IQVIA, a global provider of information, innovative technology solutions and contract research services focused on the healthcare industry', the first and only Marie Soutter who came up on a search on Google. One of the consequences of the internet and social media is that everybody feels obliged to present him- or herself in a smiling, confident way (unless exhibiting his or her trauma), as if aware that the framer of the universe loved him or her.

Indisputably, Ivy Compton-Burnett's writing is original in style and easy to parody, and I doubt that she has had many successors. Overwhelmingly her books are cast in dialogue, and most of the characters talk in the clipped way suitable for asperity. *Manservant and Maidservant* begins as follows:

> "Is that fire smoking?" said Horace Lamb.
> "Yes, it appears to be, my dear boy."
> "I am not asking what it appears to be doing. I asked if it

was smoking."

"Appearances are not held to be a clue to the truth," said his cousin.

"But we seem to have no other."

Here straightaway is demanded exactitude of language. Moreover, the exchange points to an ancient philosophical problem. If appearances are delusive but we can know the world only though them, then what contact can we have with reality? I am not philosopher enough to answer. As I sit writing this in my garden, am I to think that the grass is not *really* green but only appears so? But it is a part of reality that it appears so to me. I do not want to say that all aspects or reality are equally real for there are madmen in the world for whom their delusions represent reality. Let philosophers, then, decide what is really real.

Horace Lamb, the first speaker, is a member of an endangered species, the landed gentry, who has no money but has married money. His cousin, Mortimer, is a hanger-on, also impoverished, who is in love with Horace's wife, as she is with him. Neither Horace nor Mortimer experience the pointlessness of their existence as a stimulus to earn a living: they have inherited the right to do nothing and intend to keep their inheritance intact. Horace lives in a large and beautiful, but uncomfortable, house. His concern over the smoking fire is not that the house will catch light, but that it is a sign of unwarranted extravagance. He is a miser, though all his money is his wife's

He and she have four children, and he is as penurious of affection as of money. His asperity terrifies his children. He denies them ordinary little pleasures when there is no need for him to do so. He is not an attractive character: he is even detestable.

But one day his wife takes a prolonged absence to look after her own aged parents, and Horace suffers a slight illness. His attitude to life changes. He becomes more affectionate and indulgent towards his children, but it is too late. His hardness has entered their hearts: it is when they are very young that children need most to be loved. When Horace says that he is going for a walk which will take him over a short bridge spanning a ravine, his sons omit to tell him — accidentally-on-purpose — that the bridge has been condemned as unsafe. At least momentarily, the children wish him dead, though in the event he does not die.

Quite unexpectedly in the midst of all the narrator's asperity, there is a scene that, to me at least, is moving in a quite ordinary way. Has Ivy Compton-Burnett, then, a heart? The scene in question concerns Miss Buchanan, who runs a small shop in the village near to the house. Her shop also acts as a poste-restante that receives all the letters that the locals do not want known to the postman, to their relatives or their neighbours. In a small village, news gets round fast.

It can seldom be said that there is a key to a human personality, but there was one to Miss Buchanan's. She spent her youth at a time when education was available to young girls, but was not compulsory, and her parents preferred her help in the house to her ultimate good. The result was that she could not read and lived the rest of her life in fear that the truth might emerge. She conducted all her transactions with wariness and distance. She preferred to remain a single than to marry a husband who would know of her secret, and likewise solitude to the possession of friends who might suspect it.

This is tragic, and very far from implausible; in fact, it is finely observed. I knew a person well who devoted her life to, and deformed it by, preventing any knowledge of the fact that she suffered from anorexia nervosa and that she was not eating properly. And I once had a patient whose father committed suicide when he could not avoid having to fill in a form in someone else's presence, when it would have become clear that he could neither read nor write.

Later in the novel, on the penultimate page, Miss Buchanan's secret is publicly revealed (though by some it was already privately known), Nobody blames her: it does not have the consequences that she has spent her whole life fleeing. Bullivant, Horace's manservant, in effect offers to teach her to read, saying that it would be easy for her to learn. Miss Buchanan says:

> "Illiterate I have lived. Illiterate I will die. The time for remedying matters is past."

This has a piercing quality of suffering and regret, the realisation that time's arrow flies in one direction only and that not everything — indeed, not much — is reparable. I was reminded of my time in Paris during the *confinement* (the lockdown) in response to the Covid epidemic. One was permitted an hour out of one's residence per day, and not more than a kilometre in distance. If one sat on a public bench, it had to be at a distance from anyone else. One had to carry a form stating where one lived, and at what time one had left home.

One day, I sat on a public bench and an African came and sat at the other end of it. '*Bonjour, mon frère*,' he said to me. '*Bonjour, monsieur*,' I replied, trying not to sound cold.

He was a Malian, aged 40, who had come to France illegally ten years before. He had worked nine years in what is called 'the informal sector', or 'on the black', but now had no work. He wanted one day to return home to see his mother before she died. He now had his *permis de séjour*, which he proudly showed me, having received it shortly before.

He told me that he could neither read nor write. An illiterate illegal immigrant! How easy unmercifully to exploit!

'I could teach you,' I said. 'It's not too late for you to learn.'

'No,' he said. 'It's too late.'

Could I have taught him? I don't know and never will know: but what strange and unexpected associations reading brings, and what pleasure (or sorrow) such associations bring!

Ivy Compton-Burnett's father, James Compton Burnett (Ivy added the hyphen to give the name a more aristocratic or upper-class redolence, though her family was of quite humble ancestry), was a doctor. I was about to write 'like the father of many writers,' but my conscience, deeply affected by evidence-based medicine, gave me pause. Many doctors compared with what or whom? How many writers would you expect to have had doctors as fathers? It is enough to give examples — Dostoyevsky, Flaubert, Proust, Auden, spring to mind — to establish the point, at least if you want your point to be interesting. But if you want it to be true, you must try to show that having a doctor for a father is conducive to a literary career: it is precisely this, however, that is difficult to prove. First one would have to define who qualifies as a writer — not, presumably, any old scribbler — and then compare the parentage of writers with some other group or population. But which? Are lawyer-fathers more propitious to a child's literary career than doctor-fathers? To say so would require knowing the ratio of lawyers to doctors in the population. One would expect, prima facie, more writers to emerge from the educated classes than the uneducated, but so what? This is not an invariable rule; but even if you had your answer, what would you do with it? The question is not uninteresting, however, which proves that interest does not derive entirely from practical utility. But the demand that all prestigious occupations be distributed equally between social classes is a utopian curse of our time, a pretext for ever-greater bureaucratisation.

Be that as it may, Ivy Compton-Burnett's father was a doctor and a prolific medical writer. He studied in Vienna, then one of the leading centres in the world, if not *the* leading centre, and then in Glasgow. He became a homeopath, or 'converted to' homoeopathy, as homoeopathic writers revealingly put it, as if schools of medicine were religions. Dr Compton Burnett's London practice was both large and successful: he consulted in Wimpole Street, then as now at the heartland of the British medical elite.

Among his books was *Gout and Its Cure*. It is a small book, but at least in its second edition of 1900, the first dated 1895, expensively printed and bound. I have both the book and the disease.

Dr Burnett describes the gouty temperament:

> Your thoroughly gouty individual may have himself well in hand, and always stop to dot his I's and cross his t's, but he is at best a pent-up volcano. He may be very suave and gentle, yielding and complaisant, but that is from principle or training, or pride; *au naturel* he is a wild creature, and his subject state is the result of training.

It is true that when I was a child I had a very bad temper, and occasionally still erupt like a pent-up volcano, but rarely, and most of the time I am equable. In fact, most of the time I have nothing up with which to pent. I do not lose my temper because I have no temper to lose.

Doctors have often speculated about the temperaments specific to, or propitious for, different diseases. Before the discovery, just over forty years ago, of the bacterial aetiology of peptic ulceration, certain traits were thought to exacerbate, if not to cause, this chronic disease: traits such as ambitiousness, proneness to anxiety, and what used to be called the choleric temperament. None of this was refuted outright by the new theory, at least as far as exacerbation was concerned, for it is perfectly possible for infectious agents to affect people differentially. Therefore, the fact that Dr Burnett describes a temperament propitious to gout is not to be counted against him just because gout can now be largely prevented by pharmacological treatment.

I was rather surprised that he understood that there were

two main phases in the treatment of gout and that what he wrote in 1895 (this appeared in both the first and second edition of his book) could still be written today:

> The symptoms that precede and lead up to the uric acid retentions in the blood are a series by themselves; those due to the uric acid in the blood and which lead up to the gouty deposit attack are a second series... in the one we deal with the producing power, and in the other the product. This differentiation being made, we proceed on two lines with the treatment—the one to get rid of the gouty attack and the deposits, and the other, more important, to deal with that which leads to the production of the uric material...

Apart from the fact that gouty attacks are preceded by symptomless biochemical derangement rather than by symptoms, nothing has changed.

At the beginning of the book, Dr Burnett recounts the story of a country doctor one of whose patient's attacks of gout he always treated with port, which is usually held to be the worst of all drinks for the production of gout. (The English, especially of the upper classes, had a predilection for port, and therefore, it was often alleged, suffered the worst of all nations from gout.) The doctor treated his patient thus because he, the patient, was weak and needed 'building up'. Dr Burnett asked the country doctor whether he treated many cases of gout, to which he answered, 'Oh no, very few; people in my district are too poor to get the gout; they work too hard.' In other words, they could not have afforded the foods rich in the purines causative of gout, but now that such foods are within the reach of everyone, the prevalence of gout has increased. Indeed, it is said that 2 per cent of the adult population suffers from it. As for the country doctor himself, he suffered occasionally from gout and treated himself with oranges, 'if they are to be got.'

Citrus fruit is still held to be beneficial in gout, and the phrase 'if they are to be got' brings home just how far economic activity has expanded since the book was published. The very idea that oranges might *not* be available has become strange to us.

Dr Burnett treated his patients with many different homeopathic tinctures, including that of ladybird, in very dilute solutions (according to homoeopathic doctrine, the more diluted they were, the more powerful their action). He ascribed the recovery of his patients to his treatment, and it never crossed his mind that the recovery might not be attributable to it. But in this respect, his orthodox colleagues — or allopaths, as homoeopaths disdainfully call them — were no different. At least his nostrums were harmless, unlike many orthodox medicines, which might account for the popularity of homoeopathy, especially in illnesses that were going to get better anyway.

Was Ivy-Compton's asperity hereditary? Dr Burnett saved his for orthodox rivals. He died the year following the publication of the second edition, when Ivy was thirteen years old.

My copy has been carefully read, with little pencil ticks in the margins, where something of special importance (presumably) to the reader, or strong agreement, is noted. A patient? A homoeopathic practitioner?

No one reads Herbert Spencer (1820–1903) now, an observation made by the sociologist Talcott Parsons (1902–1979) about ninety years ago, and of whom the same might also be said. *Sic transit gloria mundi*: for Spencer in his heyday was the most famous philosopher in Europe, including Russia. Whether his eclipse was a sign of intellectual progress or something to be deeply lamented, I cannot in all conscience comment upon, for I have not read him, apart from his book of short essays, *Facts and Comments*, published in 1902, the year before his death and that in which Talcott Parsons was born. His more serious work is intimidatingly huge, and life is short, especially for me now; *Facts and Comments* contains his lighter essays but *lighter* does not necessarily mean light. Half a ton is lighter than a ton, but we still can't carry it.

The fact that Spencer had a European reputation, even when it had passed its apogee, is suggested by my copy of this book, which I think I must have bought in France, for it was evidently read by a studious Frenchman who, throughout the book and not just at the beginning of it, wrote in pencil in the bottom margins of the pages in a tiny neat hand the translations of the words that he did not know. He also put crosses at the end of lines that he thought particularly important, right or wrong. My guess is that he was a reverent disciple of a man who indeed had the appearance of an Old Testament prophet.

Insofar as Spencer is remembered today (by 0.1 per cent of

the population), it is as the originator of the phrase 'the survival of the fittest', which Darwin never used. One might assume from this that he, Spencer, was a nature-red-in-tooth-and-claw[15] man, but one would be mistaken. He was an ardent anti-militarist and anti-imperialist. His visage, however, was such as to give grim-visag'd war[16] a run for its money, and which was like the flowering of spring by comparison: a man who was more likely to explain humour than to indulge in its himself. In this last respect, he was like the doctors — more explanatory of others than indulgent themselves — who treat drug addicts.

But a man who achieved a reputation such as his could hardly have done so without merit and ability. It would not altogether have surprised him that his reputation sank almost to vanishing point soon after his death, for one of his essays, *Estimates of Men*, refers to the oscillations of men once prominent, perhaps in the awareness that his own star was waning. 'Speaking broadly,' he says, 'we may say that the world is always wrong, more or less, in its judgments of men — errs by excess or defect. Judgments are determined less by intellectual processes than by feelings; and feelings are swayed this way or that way largely by mere personal likes and dislikes, or by the desire to express authorised opinions — to be in the

---

[15] Again, not Darwin, but Alfred Tennyson, *In Memoriam*:

> Who trusted God was love indeed
> And love Creation's final law—
> Tho' Nature, red in tooth and claw
> With ravine, shriek'd against his creed.

[16] *Richard III*

fashion.' He compares the reputation of Aristotle and Francis Bacon which swing in opposite directions, and with regard to reputation Spencer concludes that 'only after numerous actions and reactions may it settle into the rational mean.' Of course, this assumes that there *is* such a mean and that no man's reputation is ever permanently damned or exalted with reason: besides which it might be questioned whether, if two and a half millennia are not enough to settle the proper estimate of Aristotle, another two and a half millennia will settle the matter.

Spencer writes a strong prose, I almost said manly, except that such would now be taken to mean toxically masculine. Here, in *Some Light on Use Inheritance* (by which he means the inheritance of acquired characteristics), he writes about the dispute between those who believe in it and those who don't:

> The parable of the motes and the beams has applications in the sphere of science as in other spheres. One striking instance of its aptness is furnished by the controversy between the neo-Darwinians and the neo-Lamarckians—to use, for the nonce, two inappropriate names. Contending for the sufficiency of natural selection, those of the Weissmann school [the neo-Darwininans] say to their antagonists—Where are your facts? To these the rejoinder made by the believers in use-inheritance may fitly be—Where are *your* facts? If one insists on inductive proof the other may also do this, and there is no inductive proof whatever of natural selection.

Whether Spencer was right or wrong (he was on the neo-

Lamarckian side of the question), this is expressed with admirable forthrightness. But of his own style, in an essay on style, he says that it was not cultivated as a style as such:

> … the sole purpose [of his writing] being to express ideas as clearly as possible and, when the occasion called for it, with as much force as may be.

Spencer's later works were dictated rather than written, and he says with genuine detachment, the following:

> Up to 1860 my books and review-articles were written. Since then they have been dictated. There is a prevailing belief that dictation is apt to cause diffuseness, and I think this belief is well-founded. It was once remarked to me by two good judges—the Leweses [i.e. G.H. Lewes and George Eliot]—that the style of *Social Studies* is better than the style of my later works, and, assuming this opinion to be true, the contrast may I think be ascribed to the deteriorating effect of dictation. A recent experience strengthens one in this conclusion. When finally revising *First Principles*, which was dictated, the cutting out of superfluous words, clauses, sentences, and sometimes paragraphs, had the effect of abridging the work by fifty pages—about one-tenth.

As an exercise, I suggest removing the superfluous words in the above quotation.

Spencer was an honest man who did not fear courting unpopularity. 'I have been repelled by the ponderous, involved structure of Milton's Prose... And from the applause of Ruskin's style I have dissociated on the grounds that it is too self-conscious—implies too much thought of effect.' This judgment was not the way to the hearts of the literati of his time.

Independent of mind, he courageously attacked my-country-right-or-wrong patriotism that was prevalent in his day. I quote two passages:

> Were anyone to call me dishonest or untruthful he would touch me to the quick. Were he to say that I am unpatriotic, he would leave me unmoved. 'What, then, have you no love of country?' That is a question not to be answered in a breath.

Having given reasons to be proud of his country — all political, incidentally, none civilisational — he gives those for shame or at least sorrow:

> Contemplation of the acts by which England has acquired over eighty possessions—settlements, colonies, protectorates, &c.—does not arouse feelings of satisfaction. The transactions from missionary to resident agents, then to officials having armed forces, then to punishment of those who resist their rule, ending in so-called 'pacification'—these processes of annexation, now gradual and now sudden... with no more regard for the wills of the inhabiting people than for those of the inhabiting beasts—do not excite sympathy for their perpetrators.

The fact that England was not alone in this — it was all but the norm — is no argument in refutation. Spencer is sometimes very modern despite his long eclipse.

Recently I completed a book-length study — a short book, but a book nonetheless — of one of Agatha Christie's crime novels, *They Do It with Mirrors*, chosen at random from those in my possession but which I still had not read. I was fortunate in my choice, not because it was one of her best books, which decidedly it was not, the plot being preposterous, but because it illustrated well my thesis that Agatha Christie was not only highly intelligent and well-informed but a social satirist of some distinction. Of course, she never thought of herself as anything more than middlebrow, and indeed her work has been attacked precisely on these grounds. The famous American critic, Edmund Wilson, said that one simply cannot read a book by Agatha Christie, by which he meant that, while one can skate over the pages and turn them over, one cannot pay any real attention to them, wishing only for the elucidation of the puzzle. I wanted to demonstrate that he was mistaken: not perhaps a very important task but one which might serve as a caution against snobbery, including my own.

I once heard a writer, whose wit and intelligence I much respected, say that while snobbery was a vice, it was a minor one, more a peccadillo than a sin.

With this I could not agree. It is my experience that the disdain of one person for another, especially when it is unfounded and based on nothing more than social prejudice, enrages people more than practically anything else, even severe injustice. Snobbery when openly expressed rather than merely felt is disdain that wounds, often lastingly. No doubt the resentment it engenders is often excessive and has its own dishonesties: a resentful person may justify his failure or bad behaviour ever afterwards because he was once the object of disdain or snobbery. But the fact remains that one should not wound unnecessarily, which snobbery often does.

I hope that my praise of Agatha Christie is not excessive, though it seems to me a considerable literary achievement to convey to scores, perhaps to hundreds, of millions of readers around the world a social atmosphere and way of life that is not their own, and interest them in it. But I have been so influenced by evidence-based medicine that when I praise or dispraise anything or anybody, I ask myself the question, 'Compared with what?'

By what standards is a writer such as Agatha Christie to be judged? By those of Jane Austen or Dostoyevsky (the latter, by the way, would have qualified for membership of the *Crime Writers' Association*)? She would have made no such claim herself. By the standards of other crime writers? That would seem the most reasonable. The immense number of them, however, would make any 'scientific' judgment impossible; and if she were compared with other crime writers, it would have to be with equally successful and prolific ones.

I picked up a crime novel that had long rested in a pile unread by me: W.J. Burley's *Wycliffe and the Redhead*, which I must have bought because the blurb said that one of the characters, Simon, was a shy antiquarian bookseller suspected of having murdered his assistant.

I had not previously heard of the author, but an obituary on the BBC website (he died, aged 89 in 2002) said that he had written 800 books. Since he had started to write comparatively late in life, and was a schoolteacher for much it, I found this figure intrinsically implausible, at least at first. Even if many of his books were short — and the one in my hand was more or less 70,000 words — this would have meant a total of at least 30 million words, or 2000 words a day every day for several decades. On the other hand, Anthony Trollope wrote 5000 words before going to work — words that are still in print — so that such Stakhanovite literary production is not impossible. As a philosopher once said, whatever happens must be possible.

Burley wrote a long series of crime novels — mine was the 23rd in the series. He wrote it when he was 83, by itself a feat that, just before my own 75th birthday, gave me hope of an active life for at least some years to come.

His hero-detective, a senior officer in Cornwall, is called Wycliffe, but if this book is anything to go by, he lacks any traits of character to make him memorable. If we met Miss Marple or Hercule Poirot, we should recognise them immediately; not so with Wycliffe. If we met him, we should have to ask him what he did for a living.

Is this more realistic? I am acquainted with only one senior policeman, a retired detective, and if he had not told me that that was what he had done for a living, I should not have guessed, even though he was involved in catching some of the most notorious criminals of his day. But is the quality of realism automatically one of praise in this kind of literature? Memorability surely requires some departure from likelihood, though not so great as to make the temporary suspension of disbelief impossible. If I were asked to describe Wycliffe, I should be hard put to do so: a respectably married man, hardworking, mildly unconventional in his methods, prey to doubts about having chosen the right career for himself, of slightly scholarly propensities. None of this makes him memorable.

His location, on the other hand, is particular to him: Cornwall, a county apart (the Cornish talk of the rest of England as if it were a foreign or separate country, though I think this is something of an affectation). Cornwall is to Wycliffe what Los Angeles is to Philip Marlowe.

The book is centred on Falmouth, once a major port but now principally a tourist destination. Simon Meagor has a second-hand and antiquarian bookshop, tending more to the latter than to the former. Introverted and bookish, he is separated from his wife by whom he has two children. He is, however, a natural bachelor, more at home among dusty bookshelves than at family occasions. Six years before the story begins, he was the principal prosecution witness in a case of manslaughter. The culprit was sent to prison and committed suicide soon after his release. His daughter, the redhead of the title, believes that Meagor perjured himself at the trial and was therefore responsible for her father's suicide.

Pretending to let bygones be bygones, she comes to work for Meagor as his assistant, but really with the intention of taking revenge on him. The plot becomes very convoluted: the author, though 83, demonstrated that he had kept up with the times (1997) by including a lot of lesbianism in it. Agatha Christie would surely have been more reticent or discreet: she

51

was born 20 years before Burley, and in any case was less determined to be realistic.

Simon Meagor is a cliché, being just as one imagines antiquarian booksellers to be. This is not to say that he is unrealistic: clichés are distillations of common experience and are not inaccurate in every case. The danger of clichés is that they pre-empt experience, so that contrary evidence cannot enter the mind. Meagor is shy, socially awkward and misanthropic, and therefore I sympathise — or is it empathise? — with him. He is *in* commerce but not *of* commerce.

Burley, though, is not Agatha Christie. He has not the sharpness, the humour, the satire, the love of human quirkiness. If Agatha Christie is a lark, he is a flightless bird.

I love useless information more than the useful variety. For some reason, it inscribes itself on my memory much more easily — perhaps I have a subconscious belief that there is a probity and disinterestedness in uselessness, absent in the selfishness and almost corruption of utility.

Be that as it may, I love too an original hypothesis, especially one of my own, about a completely unimportant matter. For example, in Agatha Christie's book mentioned above, *They Do it with Mirrors*, there is mentioned in passing, not as a character and only in the third person, a psychiatrist called Sir John Stillwell, who has trained and inspired the young psychiatrist, Dr Maverick, who *is* a main character in the book. I was able (I think) to identify Sir John Stillwell as

Sir William Norwood East[17], a psychiatrist now forgotten who worked both for the Maudsley Hospital and for the Home Office, who was the author of such books as *The Medical Aspects of Crime*, *The Psychological treatment of Crime*, and a study of 4000 juvenile delinquents, the latter highly relevant to Agatha Christie's story, which takes place in a home for precisely such delinquents.

But even if I were right, even if it could be proved beyond doubt that Christie knew of Norwood East and availed herself of his work (Norwood East's profile exactly fits that of Stillwell), this would be a fact of total unimportance and insignificance — though I suppose that a philosopher might point out that, importance or significance not being a natural quality, it is, like beauty, in the eye of the beholder. But what I can say for certain is that the identification of Stillwell as Norwood East gave me great pleasure and were anyone to say that it was a very important finding, I would be mortified. In its insignificance was its pleasure.

I performed a similar feat of identification in one of Robert Louis Stevenson's horror stories, *The Body Snatcher*. In this story, four men, including the narrator, sit every night of the year in the parlour of a pub and inn, the George, in a small town in Scotland. One of them is called Fettes, a degenerate drunk who, however, gives signs of having considerable medical knowledge.

One evening, the landlord tells them that a local landowner (probably an aristocrat) has suffered a stroke while staying at

---

[17] Sir William Norwood East lived from 1872 to 1953, dying the year after the publication of *They Do It with Mirrors*.

the inn, and that a great London doctor has been called by telegram to attend him, this being possible because the of the recent extension of the railway line to the town (it has probably been torn up by now, to the great detriment of both town and country).

The great doctor is about to arrive, and the landlord of the inn lets fall his name, Macfarlane. This name has the effect of an electric shock on Fettes, who otherwise had been fast sinking into his usual drunken stupor.

Fettes and Macfarlane were at Edinburgh medical school together, though Macfarlane was a couple of years the senior of Fettes. Both were assistants to, and favourite pupils of, Dr Robert Knox, then the most famous anatomist in Europe. At the time, the only bodies legally available in Britain for dissection were those of hanged criminals, who were far too few to satisfy demand. Knox's anatomy school was private, but much preferable (in its teaching, that is) to that of the University itself. But to continue in business, the school needed a steady supply of bodies for dissection.

This was at the time of Burke and Hare, who murdered the poor to sell their bodies to Knox's school, no questions about their provenance being asked.[18] Fettes was deputed to keep the school clean and to receive and pay for the bodies as they

---

[18] This inspired the following famous ditty:

> Up the close and down the stair,
> In the house with Burke and Hare,
> Burke's the butcher, Hare's the thief,
> Knox the man who buys the beef.

Knox had eventually to flee Edinburgh.

were delivered, usually in the middle of the night.

It must have been obvious that many of the bodies were victims of murder. Each of them was worth in the region of £7000 in today's money, such that corpses were the economic equivalent of cocaine or heroin today. Fettes averted his mind from the obvious, but Macfarlane, his senior, insisted on drawing his attention to it. One day, a man called Gray with whom they dined the night before turned up as a corpse for dissection, but Macfarlane persuaded Fettes to be a man and say nothing about it. Gray was soon dissected beyond recognition (there was, of course, no DNA testing in those days).

The anatomy school needed still more corpses, and having heard of the burial of a farmer's wife in a remote country cemetery, Macfarlane and Fettes set out one night to exhume and steal her body. In short, after a *mise-en-scène* of horror, the two body snatchers recognise the body they have exhumed not as that of the farmer's wife but as that of Gray, now restored to a perfect state — perfect, that is, as a corpse.

Macfarlane and Fettes subsequently followed very different paths in life. The former became a famous, respected and rich London physician, while the latter declined into alcoholism, perhaps permanently stung by his conscience. Macfarlane, by the time he meets Fettes in the inn, has put it all behind him, as though it had never happened, or at any rate was justified by the conditions and exigencies of the time, a mere stage in a successful career.

The story was first published in 1884. I think it is clear that Macfarlane was Sir William Fergusson, surgeon to, among others, Queen Victoria. Fergusson had indeed been assistant to Dr Knox. He left Edinburgh for London in 1840, where he was appointed professor of surgery at King's College and was soon to be full of fame and honours. But he retained his attachment to Scotland where he maintained a grand house. It was there, according to a memoir of him written after his death in 1877 for the Royal College of Surgeons by one of his colleagues, Henry Smith, 'that the first shadows of the tomb fell upon [him].' Smith wrote that 'He was the true type of a Christian gentleman, and thus... we do not lose sight of his moral worth and independence of mind.' He was what became known as 'a conservative surgeon,' that is to say, 'he cut away nothing that could be saved.' He was notable for 'his great love for preserving as much of the body as possible.'

The entry in the *Dictionary of National Biography* (copied virtually word for word by Wikipedia) makes no mention of Fergusson as the model for Mafarlane, as I think he must have been. Stevenson wrote the story in 1881, when perhaps the shadow of the tomb was too fresh for it to be published at once. In effect, if my identification is correct, Stevenson was accusing one of the great medical figures of his time of having been at the very least an accomplice to murder, if not a murderer himself. That Stevenson considered that Fergusson's activity arose from a trait of character and not from circumstance alone is suggested by his unexpected confrontation with Fettes, whom he obviously hoped never to meet again. 'A horrible, ugly look came and went across his almost venerable countenance,' wrote Stevenson.

This, to me, is fascinating — but, or because, perfectly useless.

Among the delightful but useless hypotheses the investigation of which can easily occupy a lifetime is that which suggests that William Shakespeare, the son of the glover of Stratford, was not the author of the works that were published under that name.

It was Delia Bacon, I think, who first seriously argued that Shakespeare in the second sense was really Francis Bacon. She claimed no descent from the latter, let alone communication from him, but still ended up for the last few years of her life in a lunatic asylum, dying there. Her hypothesis lived on, however, and spawned a very large number of books, of which I possess not a few: books long and short, but most of them learned in a slightly mad fashion. Among them is Sir Edwin Durning-Lawrence's *Bacon Is Shakespeare*. Durning-Lawrence was a member of parliament for eleven years, but his real interest was in the Baconian theory. For some reason, I have two copies of this book, one of which belonged to the Antarctic explorer, Sir Ernest Shackleton. I am tempted to say that he must have been a Baconian because he owned the book, but the same argument would apply to me. But did non-Baconians read Baconian literature, unless it were for the purpose of refutation, which I doubt that Shackleton ever intended to undertake?

Another member of parliament interested in the Shakespeare authorship question, as it is now called, was Sir Granville George Greenwood, who carried on a controversy with opponents even in the middle of the First World War, writing a 600-page volume, published in 1916, the very year in which hundreds of thousands, perhaps a million, were slaughtered in the Battle of the Somme. You might have thought that he had other matters on his mind just then, but the grip of the question is strong once it takes hold (his book was his second on the subject that he wrote, the first being of similar length, published in 1909). But Greenwood was not a Baconian, only an anti-Stratfordian, He did not believe that the boy from Stratford could have written the works attributed to him, but he did not attribute them to anyone else. In the language of the searchers after the true Shakespeare, the term *Stratfordian*, a believer that Shakespeare was Shakespeare, is one of contempt. For them, such a person is no better than someone who believes that the earth is flat.

During the Second World War, a retired surgeon in bath, W.S. Melsome, who is said to have known the works of both Shakespeare and Bacon by heart, and who could come up immediately with parallels between the two, wrote *The Bacon-Shakespeare Anatomy*, the war not having reduced the importance of the authorship question. There is something magnificent in this ability to ignore the horror of the times by indulging in slightly mad scholarship.

Later, Bacon fell out of favour as the main candidate, other than Shakespeare, for the authorship of Shakespeare, such luminaries as Sigmund Freud plumping for Edward de Vere, Earl of Oxford. It was, perhaps, unfortunate that the man who originated this hypothesis that Oxford was Shakespeare was a teacher by the name of Looney, but perhaps my favourite among the searchers for the true author is Dr Orville W. Owen, a Baconian.

He invented a cipher machine of great elaboration that

informed him that Shakespeare-Bacon's manuscripts were buried in a sealed chest in the river Wye at Chepstow, and having persuaded the Duke of Beaufort of the evidence for his theory, had the river dredged at great expense, largely the Duke of Beaufort's.

Alas for Dr Owen, who sunk his own money as well into the project, nothing was found except a few rotting timbers of a jetty. Ruined financially, in his deathbed he warned people against the Shakespeare authorship question. Before he took it up, he had been a prosperous doctor in Detroit, Michigan, but he left his family, which had accompanied him to Chepstow, in penury. The story recalls me to Hilaire Belloc's comic poem, *Henry King*:

> The Chief Defect of Henry King
> Was chewing little bits of String.
> At last he swallowed some which tied
> Itself in ugly Knots inside.
>
> Physicians of the Utmost Fame
> Were called at once; but when they came
> They answered, as they took their Fees,
> "There is no Cure for this Disease.
>
> "Henry will very soon be dead."

On his deathbed, Henry King:

> Cried 'Oh my Friends, be warned by me,
> That Breakfast, Dinner, Lunch, and Tea

Are all the human frame requires…'
With that, the Wretched Child expires.

Among my Baconian books is *The Mystery of Francis Bacon*, by William T. Smedley, published in 1912, at the very apogee of Baconianism. The argument is familiar. The plays must have been written by someone with an intimate knowledge of both Italy and France, and Bacon fits the bill. Moreover, it is obvious from the plays that the author must have been learned in many fields. Again, Bacon fits the bill, for all are agreed that he was phenomenally learned. Smedley quotes a non-Baconian scholar, G.G. Gervinus, who pointed out the similarities between Bacon's and Shakespeare's work which, of course, Smedley takes to prove identity:

> Both are alike in the rare impartiality with which they avoided everything one-sided… Both, therefore, have an equal hatred of sects and parties, Bacon of sophists and dogmatic philosophers, Shakespeare of Puritans and zealots. Both, therefore, are equally free from prejudices and astrological superstition in dreams and omens. Bacon says of the alchemists and magicians in natural science that they stand in similar relation to true knowledge as the deeds of Amadis to those of Caesar, and so does Shakespeare's true poetry stand in relation to the fantastic romances of Amadis. Just as Bacon banished religion from science, so did Shakespeare from Art; and when the former complained that the teachers of religion were against natural philosophy [science], they were equally against the stage.

The author quotes from *The Rape of Lucrece*, one of Shakespeare's early long poems:

> But she that never cop't with stranger eyes
> Could pick no meaning from their parting looks,
> Nor read the subtle-shining secrecies
> Writ in the glassy margents of such books...

Unusually, according to him, Bacon annotated by hand all the thousands of books that he read, and therefore the last two lines just quoted must refer to him. As to the Sonnets, the elderly Bacon (aged 49 when they were first published, which was elderly for the time) was largely addressing his younger self in them. Sonnet 62, for example, speaks of Bacon's younger self:

> Sin of self-love possesseth all min eie
> And all my soule and all my every part
> And for this sin there is no remedie
> It is so grounded inward in my heart.

The beautiful childless youth of the earlier sonnets is the younger Bacon, and therefore Shakespeare *is* Bacon, as Durning-Lawrence had said.

On *Wikipedia*, William T. Smedley is entered as an American engraver, portrait painter and watercolourist who also wrote *The Mystery of Francis Bacon*. This seemed to me very strange. How did a prolific artist also have time to study the arcana of Elizabethan bibliography, mastery of which is displayed in the book?

The answer is that William T. Smedley, the artist, was not the William T. Smedley who wrote *The Mystery of Francis Bacon*. There was a William T. Smedley who was an ardent British collector of Elizabethan books, many of which he sold to the Folger Library in Washington.

The artist William T. Smedley lived from 1858 to 1920. The bibliophile William T. Smedley lived from 1851 to 1930, seventeen years longer. William Shakespeare lived from 1564 to 1616, Francis Bacon from 1560 to 1625, thirteen years longer. This proves something, but goodness knows what.

Every little animal has its little pleasure, as the Germans say, and mine is books: not only reading them, but buying them, contemplating buying them, and owning them.

Few pleasures are greater to me than to receive a bookseller's catalogue through the post — an online catalogue is much less pleasurable. I suppose this pleasure would be alien or mysterious to most of the world's population, and I freely admit that, in my situation, it is ridiculous. I already have more books than I can read before my death (though not more than I would like to have read) and have reached an age at which those that I already possess will soon be a bother to my legatees. These days it isn't easy to give books away, let alone sell them: and a professor at Oxford has just been quoted, as I write this, as saying that young people these days — students of literature — have difficulty in reading an entire book.

A few times a year, I receive the catalogue of Jarndyce, antiquarian bookseller specialising in eighteenth and nineteenth century books. The only time I regret not being much richer than I am is when I look through these catalogues, the most desirable items being far beyond my purse. I did once splash out, however, on a first edition, still anonymous, of De Quincey's *Opium-Eater*, with an interesting letter of De Quincey's laid in. Another time, from another bookseller, I splashed out on the unexpurgated and soon to be suppressed first printing of Graham Greene's *Journey without Maps*, inscribed by the author to Antony Hobson, the eminent authority on book-collecting. I was writing a book about Liberia at the time of this folly, and for some reason thought that a copy of Graham Greene's account of his journey through that country that had passed physically through his hands would inspire me (magical thinking is never quite dead, even in a rationalist such as I). A third extravagance (relative to my means) was the purchase of a copy of Jules Cotard's paper describing the psychiatric syndrome — depression with nihilistic delusions — that is now called by his name, inscribed by him to Dr Adrien Proust, Marcel Proust's doctor-father. Cotard appears in Proust's masterwork, lightly disguised.

But to return to Jarndyce, and in particular to their latest catalogue. Their catalogues are always an aesthetic pleasure in themselves, but the latest one — *A Catalogue of Detective Fiction* — was surpassingly so. The covers of late nineteenth century books, which would once have been despised as merely Victorian, and therefore tasteless, were copiously illustrated and beautifully reproduced. There may have been progress in many directions, but not in the design and execution of the covers of crime novels, which from 1870 to the outbreak of the First World War were an art form in themselves.

Of the view from Westminster Bridge in 1802, Wordsworth wrote:

> Dull would he be of soul who could pass by
> A sight so touching in its majesty...

I would not go so far, perhaps, as to claim that this catalogue was majestic, but I would say that dull would he be of soul who could open it and not be impressed by the artwork and intrigued by the brief accounts of the authors and the summaries of the plots of their books that it contained. Such a person would not be able to say that nothing human was alien to him, rather that nothing human was of interest to him.

Not all the titles in the catalogue were of fiction: a few were of the genre now known as 'true crime'. Here, for example, is *The Man They Could not Hang*, by John Lee:

> John 'Babbacombe' Lee, 1864–1945, was sentenced to death for the murder of Emma Keyse, his employer, who was found stabbed to death at her house in Babbacombe Bay, near Torquay, in November 1884. The evidence in the case was flimsy and circumstantial, but Lee was sentenced to hang on February 23rd, 1884. Despite working perfectly well during tests, the trapdoor of the scaffold failed to open each time Lee was prepared, and after three failed attempts to execute the prisoner, the medical officer refused to take part any more. Lee's sentence was commuted to life in prison, and after many appeals he was released in 1907, after which he lived off his notoriety as 'the man they could not hang,' giving

lectures and even performing in a silent film.[19]

The implication in this passage is that the presence of a doctor was legally necessary for the procedure of execution by hanging, and that he could prevent it by refusing to take part. And while we should all feel especially revolted by any continuance of the attempt to hang Lee after three failed attempts, this revulsion is odd, inasmuch as the continuance, had it taken place, was a lesser horror than execution in the first place. (I have mentioned elsewhere that it took five attempts to hang the only man I ever knew who was executed by hanging, the Nigerian writer Ken Saro-Wiwa.)

Babbacombe was the scene of what is the second memory of my life. I must have been about four years old, and it was in the grounds of a hotel in which we were staying that a black and white dog terrified me. I took refuge in some laurel bushes and was extremely scared every time I left the hotel lest I should encounter him again.

Here is an extract from the preface to *Hunted Down* by James M'Govan, the pseudonym of William C. Honeyman, a New Zealand born Scottish author and musician who, under his own name, published a number of works of violin instruction but who was best known for his detective fiction that were believed at first to be factual:

---

[19] This potted history, as I later discovered, is not quite accurate, or at least far from the whole truth. Lee's notoriety did not survive the First World War, and he went to live quietly, though perhaps not legally, in the United States, for he would not have been allowed into the country if he had admitted to having been a convicted felon.

A writer who exalts an active cut-throat into a hero, who makes robbery appear a comic pleasantry, and the life of a thief a succession of noble triumphs, is himself a criminal — a pest to society — a scoundrel whose reward should be the hulks[20] or prisons he is helping to fill.

M'Govan published books of short stories with titles such as *Garrotted to Order, M. Sweeney Among the Body-Snatchers, Jemmy Twitcher's Patent Suicide, Poisoned Sugar* and *An Unburied Burglar*.

Arthur Morrison (1863–1945) was another author who wrote on more than one subject, most famously about the slums of the East End of London, but also about Japanese woodblock prints, in which he was a great expert. He sold 1,846 such prints to the British Museum in 1906, leaving the rest of his collection to it on his death. He invented a detective called Martin Hewitt, who was the hero of novels with titles such as *Green Eye of Goona, The Case of Mr Geldard's Elopement, The Case of the Flitterbat Lancers, The Case of the Ward Lane Tabernacle,* and *The Affair of the Avalanche Bicycle and Tyre Co, Limited*.

Somerset Maugham said that he could happily read such publications as the catalogue of the Army and Navy Stores, or Bradshaw's railway guides, rather than nothing at all, but I do not need the negative stimulus of having nothing at all to read in order to enjoy Jarndyce's catalogues.

---

[20] Prison ships moored in estuaries.

My friend Professor Ferner sent me a celebrated book for my seventy-fifth birthday, *Classic Descriptions of Disease*, by Ralph H. Major. It was the third edition, published in 1945, the first having been published in 1932. The book is exactly what the title suggests that it is (by no means all titles of books are so good a guide to their contents), namely a compendium of classic, usually first or early, descriptions of disease, combined with brief biographical notes on their authors. Such had been the rapid progress of medical knowledge in the late nineteenth and early twentieth centuries that many of the entries must have seemed rather more recent or contemporary in 1932 than they do now.

It is a heavy book both to carry and to read; it is to be dipped into rather than read from cover to cover.

Perhaps it is a sign of my susceptibility to what might be called the *selfie deformation* that I turned first to classic descriptions of a disease from which I myself have suffered, namely myxoedema, the result of prolonged thyroid deficiency.

I do not intend to write a personal clinical history, except in the barest outline. I do not know whether the following two events were causally related, but in 1976 I suffered from viral myocarditis with quite severe heart failure (the death rate from which then being between 25 and 50 per cent within five years), followed two years afterwards by hypothyroidism so severe that no thyroid hormone whatever could be detected in my blood, a dangerous state in which, if I had suffered a further viral illness, I might have slipped into a myxoedema coma from which I would not have emerged. What a loss to the world that would have been!

Sir William Gull first described myxoedema in 1873, saying, 'I am not able to give any explanation of the cause which leads to the state I have described.' He says that, 'it appears to continue uninfluenced by remedies.' However, he does call the appearance of the person with myxoedema 'cretinoid', suggesting a connection to a condition that Thomas Blizard Curling, in 1850, had in turn connected to a deficiency or absence of the thyroid gland.

When I was myxoedematous — grossly so, to judge by photographs of me at the time — I was working among endocrinologists, some of them of eminence; but as we frame our observation of, and social interactions with, people as friends, relatives, acquaintances, colleagues, etc., according to expectations, they noticed nothing. For doctors, thyroid disease is what patients have, not people with whom they are working. If it had not been for an experiment for which I volunteered to be a subject, in the course of which my *Thyroid Stimulating Hormone* (TSH) was measured, I might have died, perhaps after a period as a patient in a psychiatric ward for the demented.

Having described the physical changes of myxoedema — the thickening and coarsening of facial features, for example — Gull says:

> To those about such a patient the whole morbid condition is likely to be attributed to indolent habits, and the apparent incapacity for exertion to be deemed dependent upon mere inertness of the will. No doubt extreme circumstances have a distinct influence of these as upon other patients, but I believe the disinclination to

mental or muscular activity is largely pathological.[21]

Certainly, I attributed my own slowing down to mere laziness, a vice to which I had in any case been naturally inclined, though when I found it exhausting to climb an ordinary flight of stairs (I was only 27, remember), I began to think that something was wrong with me; but that whatever it might be was likely to be fatal and therefore there was no point in seeking medical attention. I had other things to do before I died than waste what little time I had with consulting doctors.

The link of a fault or sin — laziness — to a physical cause, in this case hypothyroidism, was moral progress that obviated much cruel censoriousness. On the other hand, it must have increased a cultural propensity to confound sin and illness (not so much that no one does wrong knowingly, but that no one does wrong healthily). If the endocrinological or other physical causes of vice and wrongdoing have not yet been found — well, remember the story of myxoedema, whose mental consequences were once also thought to be signs of moral defect.

The other essay or paper on the subject of myxoedema in *Classic Descriptions of Disease* that interested me was by George Redmayne Murray (1865–1939). He it was who, in 1891, first treated a myxoedematous patient with injections, and later with oral extracts, of sheep thyroid. In a sense, I owe my life to him — and, of course, to the sheep.

In 1920, he published a paper in the British Medical

---

[21] Note that Gull does not consider psychological causes in themselves as possibly pathological.

Journal with the biography of the first patient he treated with thyroid extract:

> When she was 41 or 42 years of age her relations had noticed that she was becoming slow in speech and action, and she herself began to find that it required a great effort to carry on her ordinary housework. The features gradually became enlarged and thickened and the hands and feet increased in size and changed in shape, so that at the time of this meeting she presented the typical facies of an advanced case of myxoedema [as did I eighty-five years later] of at least four years' duration... She complained of languor, a disinclination to see strangers and great sensitiveness to cold... The experimental nature of the treatment was explained, and the patient, realizing the otherwise hopeless outlook promptly consented to this trial... She enjoyed excellent health until early in 1919... This patient was thus enabled, by the regular and continued use of thyroid extract, to live in good health for over twenty-eight years after she had reached an advanced stage of myxoedema. During this period she consumed over nine pints of thyroid extract or its equivalent, prepared from the thyroid glands of more than 870 sheep.

I have lived nearly 50 years with thyroxine (not prepared from sheep, however).

Between Gull's paper in 1873, then, and Murray's first use of thyroid extract, much must have been elucidated about myxoedema. No doubt if Murray hadn't tried it, someone else would have done so; nevertheless, it was *he* who was first. He needed no controlled trial to establish the worth of the treatment because it was 100 per cent certain that without it the course of the patient's life would have been downhill. That she survived for 28 years in good health was proof enough.

Not so with the trial of streptomycin, the first truly effective drug against tuberculosis. The course of this disease was so variable that it was easy to attribute an improvement in any individual case to whatever treatment he or she had been given, rather than to chance and spontaneous change. Therefore, a controlled trial was necessary to establish the worth of any proposed treatment. The first trial of this type in history was of streptomycin. Among those who co-operated in this trial (which was successful) was Dr R. Shoulman, who once owned the book given me by Professor Ferner. The very long paper reporting the trial was published in 1948; Dr Shoulman remained a researcher in the field of tuberculosis, a field then of declining importance but now, unfortunately, of increasing importance again. In 1971 he published, with others, a paper on the Heaf Test which helped to distinguish between active and dormant tuberculosis.

The difference in the methodology necessary to prove the efficacy of thyroid extract and streptomycin was interesting (to me, at least), all the more so because we seem to have entered an era of methodological rigidity and dogmatism.

Two tiny footnotes. Sir William Gull was the doctor who first gave the name *anorexia nervosa* to that condition. He was suspected by some to have been Jack the Ripper, an idea I found preposterous because, among other reasons, he was 71 years old at the time of the Whitechapel murders, which were surely the work (if that is quite the word for it) of someone younger.

As for George Redmayne Murray, he served as a medical adviser in Italy during the First World War — in which two of his three sons were killed.

Are poets born or made? — or something in between the two, which is more likely? At any rate, it is certain that I have no poetic gift. I have occasionally thought of the first line of a poem — it always comes to me in a flash of inspiration — but the second will not come, though whether this is from lack of capacity or persistence I cannot say. I have no poems to my name; my second lines of poetry are as rare as the second editions of my books.

Vernon Scannell (1922–2007) was a prolific poet, sometimes decried both for his facility and accessibility. He denied that he wrote easily and said that he wrote with great care. His view was that difficulty in poetry should lie with the poet, not with the reader, and he was at one with A.E. Housman about how poetry should have an emotional impact rather than be an intellectual puzzle: and to move, it must be comprehensible, even if it can later yield up latent meanings.

Must a poem move, or move most, at first reading? There ought to be something that appeals immediately, otherwise we would never return to it; but less obvious or evident meanings may subsequently reveal themselves, and emotional responses deepen. Moreover, precise meaning is not always discernible, any more than is the shape of a mist. But just because the shape of a mist is not discernible does not mean that the mist has no limit, much less that it does not really exist. Words can move us more when their meaning is translucent rather than transparent. A French academic who specialised in English poetry (or poetry in English) once said, on hearing a poem of Dylan Thomas's for the first time, 'I don't understand it, but I know that it's magnificent.'

I do not think that any of Vernon Scannell's lines sticks in the mind as a burr to cloth, as do some of Thomas's, but he is still worth reading. Do all poets hope that their lines will be remembered — memorised — or is it enough for them to be read? For a poet to be considered great, must his lines be not only memorable but remembered, at least by a sufficient number of people? It would be an interesting exercise to find someone in the street who knew a line of Scannell's poetry. Perhaps, seventeen years after his death, we should be lucky within twenty minutes to find someone who had even heard of him. *Sic transit gloria mundi*.

But Scannell had a gift for transmuting the ordinary into poetry. In one of his best-known collections — once best-known, I mean — he tackles subjects that are not normally those of poetry, for example an encounter with a life-insurance salesman, in a poem titled *I'm Covered Now*. Life insurance, after all, is not merely an unusual subject of poetry, it is a subject inimical to it. In those days, from 1962 to 1965, when the poems in this collection of 68 pages were written, there were still door-to-door insurance salesmen whom it might be difficult to get rid of once they had a foot in the door. Scannell turns the embarrassment that causes people to buy insurance from such salesmen when they don't really want it into graphic verse. The false bonhomie of the salesman of that time, his equally fake reasonableness, is perfectly caught in the first lines:

> 'What would happen to your lady wife
> And the little ones—you've four I think you said—
> Little ones, I mean, not wives, ha-ha—
> What would happen to them if...' And here
> He cleared his throat of any reticence.

The change from bonhomie to reasonableness is complete:

> '... if something happened to you? We've got to face
> These things, must be realistic, don't you think?
> Now we have various schemes to give you cover.
> And, taking in account your age and means,
> This policy would seem to be the one...'

This works perfectly as social observation, prose and poetry, the rhythm of ordinary and even banal speech is beautiful. Scannell has the eye of a novelist and the ear of a poet. The reader or the listener to a recitation is as a fly on a wall. Not only that, however; he enters the mind of the poor purchaser, or victim, caught in a spider's web of rhetoric and social obligation. Referring to the salesman, Scannell, in the first person, says:

> His was an indoor art and every phrase
> Was handled with a trained seducer's care.
> I took the words to heart or, if not to heart,

Some region underneath intelligence…

The narrator buckles:

'… my limbs were weakening…'
At last I nodded, glazed, and said I'd sign,
But he showed little proper satisfaction.
He sighed and sounded almost disappointed,
And I remember hearing someone say,
No Juan likes an easy lay.

Recently I had a somewhat similar experience. I was waylaid
as I left a supermarket by a collector for a charity. With my
shopping bag full of what were mainly luxuries — women
shop for necessities, men for luxuries — I could hardly have
claimed to be penniless, and the charity was in a good cause,
or at least, was nominally so. Britain, however, has become so
corrupt — all in perfect legality — that nothing is as it seems
or is claimed to be, and charities are as crooked as the worst
of commercial companies. But the man who buttonholed me
was so persuasive, or at least insistent, that despite my
scepticism as to the value or probity of modern charities, I
donated, more from a desire to escape from him and from my
own embarrassment than from any charitable feelings.[22]

With great empathy, Scannell invests the banal with depth

---

[22] At least the charity to which I donated derived most of its
income from private legacies, unlike many modern 'charities' that
derive their income largely or wholly from the government. On the
other hand, it spent 41 per cent of its income on raising further
income, presumably on professional fund-raisers.

and even tragedy. A child's game of hide-and-seek, so pleasurable and innocent, proves an intimation of the inevitable grief of separation or abandonment:

> Call out. Call loud: 'I'm ready! Come and find me!'
> The sacks in the toolshed smell like the seaside.
> They'll never find you in this salty dark,
> But be careful that your feet aren't sticking out.
> Wiser not to risk another shout.

How well I remember precisely this, sixty-five years ago! But after a while, the searchers give up: they seem to have forgotten that they are searching, and therefore all about the child who is hiding:

> Out of the shed and call to them: 'I've won!
> Here I am! Come and own up! I've caught you!'
> The darkening garden watches, Nothing stirs.
> The bushes hold their breath; the sun is gone.
> Yes, here you are. But where are they that sought you?

The child's victory, his triumph over everyone else in the game, turns to dust and confronts him with his own unimportance or nothingness. His sudden loneliness seizes us in our heart.

I read Vernon Scannell's novel, *The Fight*, before I knew much of his biography. I knew that he had been a soldier during the war, had deserted, and then been wounded during the D-Day landings, that he had been for a short time a professional boxer, and that his life had been colourful, comprising alcoholism, many affairs, and some violence to women, but before knowing even this little I had assumed that he was a man of great refinement, so sensitively tuned seemed he to be to the suffering of others. Could so empathetic a man have led so rackety a life?

The Fight is a novel set in the world of boxing as it was in 1953, when Scannell was 30. Besides having been a boxer himself, he remained a fan of the so-called noble art all his life. And, as one might expect of so talented a writer, he managed as no one else (at least, known to me) to convey what it is, exactly, that is noble about the art. Perhaps one should call it the heroic art, rather, for it certainly calls for heroism — bravery carried much further than usual — to choose it as a profession, or even as a hobby. Heroism is not incompatible with stupidity, of course.

The main characters in the novel are Dobson, a boxing journalist and aspiring poet (as was Scannell at the time, though he was less degenerate than Dobson, still being in possession of his own teeth, unlike Dobson); Sid Gregory, a well-to-do but grubby and unattractive boxing promoter; his prostitute-turned-companion 'wife', Tina; an up-and-coming boxer called Johnny Blake; and a British middleweight champion of only moderate ability called Dave Sloane, who dies in his effort to win the world championship from the American negro boxer, Babe Simon, the best boxer in the world.

All the characters in the book refer to Babe as 'the nigger', no doubt a true reflection of the language of the time. The word, by no means a compliment, it being always assumed that blacks were at a lower level of humanity than whites, did not carry quite the same charge of insult as it would today, when only an unreconstructed racist would use it — apart, that is, from American blacks themselves, whose use of it is ironical. Babe Simon is as much the object of admiration as of contempt, but only because he differs from the supposed average of his race.

Knowing — having been part of — the milieu, Scannell, through the eyes of his aspiring boxer, describes the attraction of boxing to the working-class boy of his time. He, Johnny Blake, looks around him on the London underground in which he is travelling to a fight:

> Looking at his fellow-passengers, the shop-assistants making their plans for the evening and the office clerks and the workers absorbed in their newspapers, Johnny felt for them a curious mixture of envy and contempt. One part of him, the timorous, that could at times flame into huge and explicit fear, coveted their obvious equanimity; but the ambitious and adventurous part of his nature and his physical vanity fought hard to struggle with the importunate and despicable other self. These people, he told himself, were only half alive. The readers of newspapers, the pen pushers and shop walkers; their idea of excitement was a trip to the theatre or football match...

Opportunities to distinguish themselves were few for working-class boys in the early 1950s who had some, but not too much, imagination, and boxing was one of them. I suppose the equivalent today would be drug-dealing.

It is easy to assume that anyone connected with the sleazy business of boxing must himself be sleazy. As Scannell writes, through his character of the boxing journalist:

> … many managers were business men of a particularly unsavoury kind, receiving more or less large sums of money for which a dangerous and skilful job was performed by others. They were as bad as pimps, really, whoremasters; worse than the ordinary commercial middlemen, because their merchandise was human and susceptible to suffering.

Note here the common prejudice against middlemen, as if they were mere parasites, productive of nothing. Who has not on occasion felt such prejudice? But economies that have tried to do without middlemen, where they have been persecuted, have not only found them to be ineradicable in one form or other, but have not been conspicuous successes, to say the least. Production without middlemen has been found to be pointless, a mere fetish.

According to Scannell, however, not all boxers or managers were of bad character. In those days, the working class, or a large part of it, cleaved to a strict code of morality and lusted for respectability, whose loss was feared, when to be considered 'common' was degrading. The word 'common' is never used in this meaning today — vulgar, low-class, coarse — because the fear of being common has changed into an ambition to identify with the marginalised.

Scannell speaks from experience:

> There is perhaps no community of people with a more
> fiercely upheld and more inflexible code of sexual
> behaviour than the humblest section of the British
> working class... Its roots are planted in superstition; it has
> been nourished by religion and possesses a mythology of
> its own; and its vigour and authority have been
> maintained because of its demonstrable practicability.

This, of course, is now a world, a universe, away. But Dave
Sloane, the British champion, is a product of that culture: he
is clean, decent, uxorious, and ambitious within the strictest
moral limits.

Did such men exist? I was once inclined to believe that they
did not: how could they, inhabiting that sleazy world of sweaty
gyms and chronic gamblers? But in the 1970s, I had a patient,
a recently widowed woman whose husband had been a
champion boxer in the 1920s and 30s. She was elegantly
dressed, but more than by that I was impressed by the
refinement of her manner. It was completely at variance with
what I might have expected. I was deeply impressed — no,
moved — by her obviously sincere reverence for her late
husband, who had fought more than 200 professional fights
(which would not be allowed now). Of humble birth, he was
and remained a complete gentleman, and in the days of his
greatest fame had always been modest. To say that she revered
his name, not merely through the rosy lens of retrospection,
would not be an exaggeration. He died, alas, aged 69, no great

age from my present perspective, but what in those days I considered as passing old.

I admired my patient enormously. I looked forward to her appointments, for refinement of feeling such as hers was not often to be encountered, even then. She must be long dead now, but whenever I recall her, I still have a frisson of emotion. She and her husband had known how to live, notwithstanding the world of boxing in which they had moved.

The figure of Vernon Scannell continued to intrigue me and so I bought a biography of him: perhaps the *only* biography of him. It was by James Andrew Taylor, and titled *The Walking Wounded: The Life and Poetry of Vernon Scannell.* It was published in 2013, six years after its subject's death. My copy came with an inscription: 'Dear Dad, Merry Christmas! Love Tess, December, 2013.' I think Dad must have been a literary type, for there are fastidious little pencil ticks throughout the text and not just at the beginning of it (which is more usual). Whether they indicated something of importance, something strongly agreed or disagreed with, or both, I could not make out. There is one such tick against the following sentence:

> Perhaps, too, there is a parallel between the bed that the soldiers can't get out of and the deathbed that Scannell can't get out of, and from which he is writing the poem.

The poem in question concerned a return to the poet's memories of the D-Day Landings in which he took part (and was wounded four days later). What he suffered from:

> Was *pre*-traumatic stress disorder, or
> As specialists might say, we were 'shit-scared'…

This is implicitly to say that, when it comes to fear, those who suffer it are the *real* experts on it. This is a dangerous doctrine if taken too far, making personal experience the measure of all things; but one knows what Scannell means in the circumstances and sympathises with it. No one likes to be told what his experience *really* is by someone who has not experienced something similar. When I told my heroin-addicted patients that withdrawal from heroin was not serious, certainly not by comparison with withdrawal from alcohol, at least in some cases, they always replied, 'How do you know? You haven't been through it.' Seriousness, however, is a category that depends on the point of view and is not found in non-human nature. I would always have to explain what I meant: that such withdrawal is easily alleviated and neither long-lasting nor life-threatening. They never wanted to believe me, even when they knew that what I said was true.

This biography is an excellent one; a better example of a life illuminating the work could scarcely be found. Scannell was a very impressive but equally flawed man (but perfect men don't write poetry). He was born to a violent brute of a father and a mother who never expressed any affection for her children and never came between her husband and them when he beat them unmercifully for nothing except the pleasure masquerading as anger. Not surprisingly, Scannell left home as soon as possible and married at eighteen a girl whom he had made pregnant. He abandoned her soon after and saw the child only twice in his lifetime. He then married bigamously, but in 1940 the state had other things on its mind than young bigamists, and his wife gamely claimed to be co-responsible for his bigamy.

Scannell went to be a soldier, but he was a bad one. Sent to North Africa, he claimed to have been at El Alamein, though he hadn't. He did see action, however, and deserted after a battle, an action that troubled him for the rest of his life. 'Am I a coward?' he asked himself for years afterwards. I think the answer is, 'No': he was for a short time a professional boxer and whatever else a professional boxer may be, he cannot be a coward. Besides, he deserted *after* a battle, not before or during it, and after a period of military imprisonment he was sent to serve at D-Day (because the army needed all the men it could get) and was there wounded, through his military incompetence rather than a deliberate attempt to be excused further active service. He was sent home, where he deserted again, whereupon the army concluded, with surprising insight, that he was no use to them.

He must have had considerable charisma, for after the war he lived for a time in Leeds where he met, and was admired by, bohemians, and though not a student he attended the university where he impressed its distinguished teachers of literature, among them the aristocratic Bonamy Dobrée, who helped him in his career. Though without formal qualification, Scannell became a teacher, something which would be unthinkable today, with its pandemic diplomatosis.

He remained raffish for the rest of his days. He drank heavily and was a nasty drunk, being jealous of his many girlfriends, subsequent wife and long-term lovers, to whom he was often abominably violent. The author of the biography ascribes this, in my view too generously, to post-traumatic stress disorder (PTSD). It is true that repeated traumatising experiences occurred early in his life, but the violent jealousy of drunken men does not require PTSD to be aroused. In my medical career, I saw hundreds of such jealous men, whose violence was possibly the natural consequence of desiring the exclusive sexual possession of someone while being sexually predatory themselves, and assuming that all men were as themselves. Their violence was one way to keep a lover faithful, at least for a time.

Scannell deserted the army the first time because — or at least implies that it was because — he saw soldiers after the battle going through the uniforms of their dead colleagues in the field stealing whatever they could find on them. This disgusted him; he was never a materialist in his own life and remained notably impecunious because of his devotion to his art, which was never remunerative despite the success in it that he achieved.

His life intersects with mine a little, though I feel that, by comparison with his, I have had a shamefully easy life. (Though why *shamefully*? Does one have a moral obligation to have a difficult life?) The description of the scene after the battle in which he saw the victorious British soldiers rifling through the bodies of the dead took me back sixty years. My father had an accounts clerk, Mr B....., a man more neatly dressed than anyone today, whose black shoes I recall as having been always brilliantly polished. He was the epitome of petty bourgeois respectability and was often the object of my father's completely unjustified ire. For this reason, I sympathised with him (I sometimes went in my holidays to do a little work in my father's office) and walked with him in Regent's Park during the lunch hour. As we did so, he told me two stories that have stayed with me ever since.

He was at El Alamein and towards the end of the battle, he shot a German soldier dead. He was unsure whether the soldier was trying to surrender or to kill him, and he decided in a flash, though in general he was a slow-moving man whose every motion spoke of deliberation, that discretion was the better part of humanity, and killed him. A most unimaginative man, he had been haunted by this ever since.

Being even then good at figures, his job after the battle was to count the dead. I saw him in my mind's eye, in Regent's Park, counting the passing humans, who after all were only the pre-dead in the battle of life, in his systematic way.

In those days, our currency was still divided into pounds, shillings and pence: twenty shillings to the pound, twelve pence to the shilling. Whatever else might be said against this system, it was good for the population's mental arithmetic.

Mr B..... could add up pounds, shillings and pence as he moved his finger or a ruler down an immense column of figures, much faster than anyone could enter them into the mechanical adding machines of the time. It was an impressive, if limited skill, and he never made a mistake. I regarded it as a marvel, though it was of course soon to be redundant, like many another skill. Whether it was natural or acquired I do not know, but it suited his temperament.

At about the same time, Vernon Scannell wrote a poem about this passing way of doing things. It is a poem about an

85

old clerk, titled *The Old Books*, and is written in his voice:

> They were beautiful, the old books, I tell you…
> You've no idea, you young ones with all your machines;
> There's no point in telling you; you wouldn't understand.

All this is true.

> You should have seen them, my day book and ledger.
> The unused lines were cancelled in red ink.
> You wouldn't find better kept books in the City;
> But it's no good talking…

The poem ends:

> You'll never know what it was like, what you've missed.
> You'll never know. My God, they were beautiful, the old
> books.

And Mr B.….'s books, bound in burgundy Morocco, *were* beautiful.[23]

Is it not remarkable that a man as exquisitely sensitive as Scannell, who so understood the feelings of those who had lost a world, could also break the nose of the mother of four of his children, and give her two black eyes? Mysterious are the ways of Man.

---

[23] Among many other temporary employments, Scannell was once a book-keeper for an insurance company, though not for long.

According to his biographer, Vernon Scannell was once obliged by penury to sell his books, some of which, dedicated by his literary contemporaries, were destined to become valuable. A bookseller who understood his plight took advantage of it to give him as little as possible for them. Was this hard-heartedness or just plain good business sense — or both? When is buying cheap and selling dear beyond the pale of decency?

Another person whose penury obliged him to sell his beloved books was Dic Aberdaron, of whom, I would imagine, few of my very few readers will have heard.

I celebrated, or at least marked, my seventy-fifth birthday in Aberdaron, a place dear to me and where I had similarly celebrated or at least marked, my seventieth birthday. On the wall of the entrance to the Ship Hotel, which is simple but comfortable, there was a reproduction of an engraving of this remarkable man, known as the Cambrian Linguist. Born in Aberdaron to a carpenter and sometime boat-builder, Dic Aberdaron — Richard Roberts Jones — was said by the time of his death to have mastered between fifteen and thirty-five languages and was in the process of collating a Welsh-Hebrew-Greek lexicon. It was never published, but there is no doubt that he wrote a fine Greek and Hebrew script. He was, by our standards, completely unschooled.

I have found and bought two publications about Dic Aberdaron, who lived from 1780 to 1843. The first was titled *Memoir of Richard Roberts Jones of Aberdaron in the County of*

Carmarthen in North Wales, Exhibiting a Remarkable Instance of a Partial Power and Cultivation of Intellect, which was published in London in 1822 while, therefore, its subject was still alive; and the second was titled *Dic Aberdaron the Celebrated Cambrian Linguist*, published in 1866, twenty-three years after his death in Carmarthen.

Although the title page of the first gives no author, it is by William Stanley Roscoe, a Liverpudlian broker, poet and fervent abolitionist of the slave trade, who was born two years after Dic Aberdaron and died in the same year as he. He left something to the Welshman in his will, but the latter did not survive long to enjoy it.

A group of well-wishers financed the book on subscription:

> Any profits that may arise from this publication will be applied to make a provision for the person who is the subject of it, and whose destitute situation requires the benevolent aid of those who may be disposed to afford him their assistance.

The frontispiece to this slender volume has a beautiful line drawing of Dic, who looks as if he might play Christ in a film of the Saviour's life. He is looking in a downward direction modestly but tenderly, his silky hair cascading down in a parting from his temples, his beard very *soigné*. He wears (insofar as the sketch allows one to judge) a chemise such as a romantic poet might wear.

By contrast, the picture of him on the cover of the second publication, much smaller in page size and more roughly printed, has a crude woodcut picture of him looking wild and dishevelled. He stands, absorbed in reading, almost hunched over a book, his hair long and matted, his beard overgrown, and almost certainly dirty. His clothes are ragged, and he looks as if he smelt. I had a patient who looked and dressed like him, and he smelt worse than any man (or any animal, for that matter) I have ever known. His smell preceded him like a cold front on a weather map and lingered for at least two days in the hospital corridor after he had passed down it. In the end, I insisted on consultations in the hospital garden, and one day he asked me why, of all my patients, I insisted on seeing him there. I saw no way of avoiding the truth, and told him as tactfully as possible, for it is a worse insult that you smell than that you are ugly. The next time I saw — and smelt — him, he had made some effort to clean himself up, but he was huge and fat and creviced, and to have cleansed him thoroughly would have required an industrial cleaner. I can smell him now in my mind's nose.

The second publication about Dic Aberdaron, more a pamphlet than a book, is by Hugh Humphreys (1817–1896), printer and publisher of Carnarvon. The *Dictionary of Welsh Biography* does not mention this booklet among his accomplishments, and indeed it is as shameless an instance of plagiarism as I have ever come across, repeating Roscoe's account almost word for word (changing one or two, suggesting that by this means he could claim to have written a new work). However, there is some new information, though relatively little, about Dic's life after 1822, the year in which Roscoe's book was published.

I give but one illustration of the plagiarism, from page 16 in both publications:

ROSCOE: It was not long before fresh discussions arose between Richard and his father, on account of his attachment to the study of language, and the barbarous treatment which he had before experienced was renewed.

HUMPHREYS: But it was not long fresh dissensions arose between Richard and his father, on account of his continual attachment to the study of language, and the barbarous treatment which he had before experienced was renewed.

Humphreys had laboured to add the words 'But' and 'continual' to this passage.

Richard Roberts Jones — Dic — led a wandering life and carried his books with him in the pockets sewn into his peculiar coat. These were very precious to him, the only possessions of value to him, as were Vernon Scannell's books to him. Like Scannell, he was generous if someone showed an interest in one of his books and freely gave it away.

It is a complete mystery as to how Richard Roberts Jones developed an interest in foreign languages (he found English, foreign for him, one of the most difficult to learn). Apparently, he was even able to converse in Russian, certainly in Italian and French, and he sat at the feet of orthodox Jews to improve his Hebrew. But he was interested only in the vocabulary, etymology and grammar of a language, and not at all in what anyone said or wrote in them. I suppose that he was a kind of *idiot savant* or that he suffered from what would have been called Asperger's Syndrome before it was discovered that

Asperger was something of a Nazi.[24] At the end of Roscoe's little book is given his translation of David Meldola's *Hebrew Elegy on the Lamented Death of Princess Charlotte* (printed also in Hebrew):[25]

Woe, daughter! Britannia, increase mourning!
Weeping for a woman, a princess, and a mistress!
A woman of youth: Ah! Her beauty has failed!
A voice of howling, upon a wall of breath, howl then…

I have already mentioned that the Germans say that every little animal has its little pleasure, and one of my little pleasures (I am glad to say that I have more than one) is to buy and read Victorian pamphlets and books whose pages are yellow and emit an acrid or acid smell and often have dramatic or lurid pictures on their covers. They are fragile and easily fall apart, which means that they must be read with care not only mental but physical.

I have also already mentioned John 'Babbacombe' Lee and my weak connection to the place where he allegedly committed a murder. I came by Lee's memoir, *The Man They Could not Hang*, and read it at a sitting.

It is generally assumed that Lee's memoir must have been

---

[24] He was said to have acquiesced with the killing of some children in order to save others.
[25] David Meldola (1797–1853) was acting Chief Rabbi to the Sephardic Jews of London. He was one of the founders of the *Jewish Chronicle*, which is still going strong.

ghosted, but I do not know the grounds for this assumption, except snobbery; it rests on the assumption that a man born in such circumstances as was he, with no more of an education than rural Devonshire could in those days provide, could possibly have written something for himself, let alone something as good as this. Here there is the shadow of the Shakespeare authorship question: no mere grammar schoolboy of an illiterate father from Stratford (if indeed he attended the school at all) could have become the greatest writer the world has known.

The text of Lee's memoir is about a hundred pages long and mentions no publisher, though it does give an address in Henrietta Street in Covent Garden. It is in light blue paper covers, the front of which is occupied by a picture of Lee, bound at the elbows, wrists and ankles, as if he were a live chicken about to be roasted alive, with a white hood over his head, standing on a trapdoor with a noose round his neck, while in the background the executioner, James Berry, pulls desperately at a lever that it supposed to open the trapdoor into the pit below into which Lee, his neck broken, is supposed to fall. Strangulation rather than a broken neck, a slower death, was a risk; but as we now know, he died by neither.

First the authorship question. There is an excellent historical study of John Lee's case titled, not surprisingly, *The Man They Could not Hang* (there is no copyright in titles), by Mike Holgate and Ian David Waugh, published in 2005, ninety-eight years after the first book of that title. It is an admirably thorough piece of work, and among other things prints some of the letters that Lee wrote in the twenty-three years he spent in prison after his botched execution and his sentence had been commuted to life imprisonment. These letters demonstrate that Lee was a young man of some feeling and that he was probably better able to express himself in writing than would someone of his social level today. Since he was born in 1864, and the Education Act was passed in 1870, it seems to be likely that the education that he received — 'an ordinary village lad', as he calls himself — was not primarily attributable to the state. Here he writes to his parents while awaiting execution, indeed on the very eve of it:

> Dear Mother and Father, I am now taking my pen to write to you a few lines before leaving this world and I hope you are well after your journey last Saturday... I know this is a great trial for you to bear. I know that it is harder for you than for me but we must trust in the Lord Jesus Christ and ask him to help us through this great trouble... My dear Father and Mother, I hope these lines will give you comfort. It is all I can give you in this world, and I hope you will pray to God to meet me in the next world.[26]

Written aged twenty in the shadow of the scaffold, I think he could have written his memoir unaided at the age of 43, when he was a free man.

There are so many matters of interest in this account of the case that I can mention only two of them: the first being the bone-headed and cruel inflexibility of the authorities when

---

[26] He signed the letter 'Your affectionate son', a more dignified and possibly more sincere way of ending an epistle than most twenty-year-olds could manage today, if they could manage one at all.

Lee asked them to permit his parents, who were poor and lived far away, to visit him for an hour every year rather than for half an hour every three months. This request was turned down.[27]

The second is a letter in the *Times*, to the effect that there was no good reason for a commutation of Lee's sentence to life imprisonment just because three attempts to hang him had failed. It concedes that to continue after three failed attempts might have shocked people's feelings, but:

> We submit that the question of whether people's feelings are shocked or not is of secondary importance. The essential thing is to show that the sentence of the law shall be carried out, and that untoward events may delay, they cannot be allowed to deflect it.

I do not think that anyone who read Lee's account of what happened would be long of this opinion:

> Let me now tell you all about the first attempt made to hang me.
> As soon as I was in position the executioner stooped down and fixed a bolt round my ankles.
> I looked about once more. Rising up in front of me was

---

[27] On the rear cover of Lee's book is an advertisement for Fry's Fine Concentrate Cacao. A young lady in a very full dress with a shawl and a large beribboned hat, is enjoying a sup of cacao. 'By making Fry's Pure Concentrated Cacao your staple beverage at Breakfast, Lunch and Supper, you really drink in health. It builds up the body and helps to resist weather-changes and dampness.'

a dreary prison. At one of the windows I could see the reporters wating to see how I would die. There were some birds hopping about in the gardens near the [scaffold] shed. How sweet this music was…

I was soon brought back to the morning's dreadful reality. While Berry was making his preparations, the chaplain, Mr Pitkin, who, of course, was robed, came and stood just outside the shed and in front of me. He was still reading the burial service. He seemed to be much affected. His voice trembled as he read.[28]

I felt the belt being pulled tight at my ankles. Next Berry put a big bag over my head. It was like a pillow-case, except that it had elastic just where it fitted round the neck.

I had, I thought, looked my last on the light of day.

No qualms of soul tormented me. I was perfectly conscious of all that was passing.

As I was wondering what would happen when the moment of death arrived, I felt something being placed round my neck.

It was the rope.

For the moment I was conscious of a strange sensation in my throat. My mouth went dry. I could feel the executioner's fingers about my neck. I felt him pull the rope tight, so that it pinched me under the left ear.

As he jerked the rope into position, Berry asked me if I had anything to say.

---

[28] A burial service for a man still alive and perfectly healthy but soon to be dead, all within his own hearing, must surely be a fearful thing.

"No," I replied. "Drop away."

I held my breath and clenched my teeth. I heard the chaplain's voice.

I heard the clang of the bell. I heard the wrench of a bolt drawn and –

He continues his account:

My heart beat. Was this death? Or was it only a dream? A nightmare?

What was this stamping going on?

Good Heavens! I was still on the trap! It would not move!

"This is terrible," I heard someone say.

After an amount of stamping caused the trap door to open, Lee was taken away, his hood removed. Then the whole thing was repeated a second and a third time, with the same result.

But was Lee guilty of the murder? He might have been; he might have been an accomplice; or he might have been a witness before or after the fact who preferred to die than speak out; or he might have been entirely innocent. What can be said for certain is that he should not have been found guilty.[29]

From John 'Babbacombe' Lee to Boris Johnson is something of a leap. I had been asked to write about the latter's memoir,

---

[29] Though the death penalty had been long abolished by the time I was a prison doctor, there was still a chamber in the prison called *the topping shed*.

Unleashed, a task that I did not relish, not only because I knew very little about him despite having met him a few times (or *because* I had met him a few times). He was both amusing and prepared to be amused — a rarer quality — but I was not sure that he was a man I should entirely trust, not because he was bad, but because he was inconstant.

Knowing little about him, I decided to read a few books about him before embarking on his tome of 750 pages. I did not want to rely entirely on his own account of events.

One of the books concentrated entirely on his fall from office. I thought it ill-written (it infuriates me, pedant that I am, when a writer uses *disinterested* for *uninterested*, because the distinction, which is an important one, will be lost, to the impoverishment not only of the language but of thought itself), and the day-to-day details of petty political intrigue do not much interest me. It made mention of many minor politicians who remained mere names to me, without any personal characteristics for my mind to hold on to. I would have found a book about postage stamps of greatly more interest.

Still, I read it from cover to cover, for I always fear to miss something of vital importance in the last twenty pages. But though there were no great revelations in the book, there was nevertheless something that, to my displeasure, I learnt from it, namely the extremely low intellectual and cultural level of our senior civil servants and the senior advisers who surrounded Boris Johnson — at least, if they were represented fairly in the book.

The people by whom the Prime Minister was surrounded, or by whom he chose to surround himself, seem to have two modes of speech: polysyllabic managerialese and vulgar expletive. Of genuine humour there was none, nor did they say anything memorable or wise. Everything suggested mediocrity, even militant mediocrity, though mediocrity combined with vaulting ambition.

On scores of pages, we find expressions such as 'Fuck! Fuck! Fuck!' and 'We're fucked.' According to the author, who spent many hours interviewing the people concerned, Members of Parliament, civil servants, government advisers, of whom there seemed to be whole flocks, talked like this. When it is not fuck, it is shit, as in 'Shit, they may not even be able to get through tomorrow' [that is, without too many resignations to continue in office]. But shit comes a poor second to fuck, for example:

> As soon as she landed, I knew we'd fucked up.
> It was a case of 'the fuckers are not going to throw me out the door.'
> That's your job, you're the Cabinet Minister in charge, so go and fucking do it.
> Tom Blenkinsop… told him to 'fuck off.'
> One senior Tory MP asked a colleague 'What the fuck is wrong with these people?'

The word and its cognates are not very expressive, even as intensifiers. 'What the fuck is wrong with these people?' means nothing different from 'What is wrong with these people?' — or, for that matter, from 'What the fuck is fucking wrong with these fucking people.'

We have to pinch ourselves to remind us that we are here speaking of an elite, or at least the people who are on the top of the pile — or, as they would no doubt put it, 'the fucking pile.'

As it happens, on the day I started to write this, I received my weekly copy of the *Spectator*. There was in it a review of a book about book curses — the imprecations that people used to write in books to dissuade or punish those who borrowed but did not return books. It begins as follows:

> 'I could lend you my copy, but the fucker who previously borrowed it still hasn't given it back.' These precise words were uttered to me by an eminent churchman... while chatting at high table about a book he believed I might find useful.

This is not exactly out of Anthony Trollope. The question arises, at least in my mind, as to why an elite now finds it expedient to use such language. (If it is not an elite in all senses, it is certain that it is not in the lowest decile, quintile, quartile or half of the population, socio-economically speaking.) What, then, is the reason or explanation for this vulgarisation of language, so inexpressive, unnecessary and indeed unnatural in the sense that it is quite deliberate and did not start spontaneously?

I suspect that it began with a loss of cultural confidence and the former elite's loss of belief in its own legitimacy. The idea that there should exist any elite at all became almost taboo, an idea that one could not utter in polite (that is to say, in elite) company. However, just because the idea of an elite becomes reprehensible does not mean that those who reprehend it do not want themselves to be, or to remain, an elite. Such people live in a state of what psychologists call cognitive dissonance (they were once known as hypocrites). They think they should not want what in fact they do want.

One method of solving this seeming contradiction is to appear to be of lower social class than the one to which they either belong to or aspire to belong to. If the lower orders use coarse or vulgar language, then by aping it the aspiring or existing elite demonstrates that it is not different from them and is therefore not really an elite at all, while at the same time retaining all its privileges both social and economic.

This view of the lower social orders is not very flattering. As I write this, there live next door but one to me a couple, born in 1940, who were brought up in really impoverished proletarian homes, but homes in which the bad language to which I have referred was anathema and would have been punished if used. By dint of hard work and intelligence they escaped their circumstances, but never for a moment did they think it liberated them from the obligation to suppress bad language in their own children or give them licence to use it. They do not even think in bad language.

One of Boris Johnson's attractive qualities, it is said, is his tolerance, his uncensoriousness. I think this is probably right. But is it not at least possible that the desire to avoid censoriousness can go too far and that, if taken too far, it can lead to a collapse of all standards of propriety, even the idea of propriety itself?

It's only a matter words, you might say. Yes, but every resort to the word 'fuck' obviates the need to be more verbally precise, and therefore for thought itself. The absence of real thought was only too obvious in senior figures portrayed in the book.

What's the good of a book without pictures, said Alice, and Mao Tse-Tung might have agreed. One picture, he said, is worth a thousand words — especially, he might have added, if they were his.

I used to be contemptuous of books largely, or solely, consisting of pictures, but I have softened my stance somewhat. Books of photographs of historic events, for example, can tell you a lot and give you great insight, though not necessarily in nuanced fashion. Like words, photographs have to be chosen, and like words they can be cropped, edited, falsified and torn out of context, and the intentions of those who took them can be manipulated to their precise opposite. However, one cannot be sceptical of everything, for the idea of falsification is parasitic upon that of truth. No one disbelieves everything.

While in Dublin for the day, I visited the Secret Bookshop, which is down a narrow passageway and where cheap remaindered books are sold, as well, unfortunately, as records and compact discs, played at a volume to strip your scalp from your skull. It discourages you from lingering and encourages quick decisions. I escaped as soon as I could with a book of photographs titled *Red-Color News Soldier*, which had a red plastic cover reminiscent of Mao's little red book of boring clichés that millions of de-cerebrated people brandished aloft during the Great Cultural Revolution, whether voluntarily or involuntarily: not only in China, incidentally. How well I remember from those days the *Little Red Book*, held up like poppies in a field, agitated as proof of loyalty and conformity in China as a kind of talisman against epidemic oppression.

The book I bought was quarto size and was comprised of the photographs of Li Zhensheng taken during the Cultural Revolution with little text. He was a photographer in Harbin, in northern China, when the Cultural Revolution broke out, in which, as a loyalist, he at first believed. Gradually, however, he came to see the importance of photographing the events as an historical record of vicious madness, and of preserving the photographs for posterity. This required laudable independence of mind, especially given the terrifying hysteria and menacing conformism by which he was surrounded. He was a real hero without, as far as I know, ever having claimed to be such.

There have been other instances of political mass hysteria, but few affecting so many millions. Li Zhensheng did not photograph many deaths, the exception being that by public execution of four ordinary criminals and two so-called class enemies, but he captured something that affects our imagination even more and is important precisely because ideologues in the West would like to impose watered-down versions of the Cultural Revolution in order to purge the minds of the recalcitrant of their incorrect ideas. How they would like there to be held public confessions, struggle sessions, and the like! Re-education camps, in the form of team-building weekends, exist already.

It is true that one picture can say a great deal, occasionally all that needs to be said. For example, there is one of Deng Guoxiang, supposedly a rich peasant, bowing low, in abject misery, before a vast crowd in Harbin. One sees him only from the side, but he wears a padded jacket so torn that it is hardly more than rags. The crowd in range of the camera looks into the camera blankly, as if exhausted, rather than at the wretched scapegoat, who is the object of a struggle session. On the very next page is Yuan Fansiang, dirty and dishevelled, also a model of abjection as he is accused of deviation by a local woman, Chiu Xihua. One trembles for humanity.

The human cruelty of the Cultural Revolution would beggar belief if it were not for human history. Ouyang Qin was the former Party Secretary of Heilongjiang province and was a target of the Red Guard. Fortunately for him, he had studied in France with Chou En-Lai in the 1920s, and Chou protected him by having him transferred to a military hospital. His son, Ouyang Xian, made the fatal mistake of writing an anonymous letter to the provincial revolutionary committee defending his father, and his writing was recognised. He was arrested and spent several days in a 'struggle session', held in a demeaning position and then having a glove stuffed in his mouth to prevent him from proclaiming his father's innocence (others had their jaws dislocated to achieve a similar end). He is surrounded by hundreds of people, those nearest to him straining to join in the obligatory abuse, some of them obviously enjoying themselves.

How easy it is to join a crowd in practising cruelty, and how difficult not to join in! This is so even when there is no official penalty for refusal, but where political fear is added to social pressure it is all but impossible. One can praise heroism when it occurs but not require it.

Accompanying the pictures is a short memoir by the

photographer. His first serious girlfriend, whom he loved and intended to marry, separated from him because she knew that their liaison would ruin his career.

> After graduating, she [San Peiku] had been selected as a model teacher by both the municipal and the provincial authorities, but during the Cultural Revolution her mother was condemned for being brought up in a landlord family and, tormented, committed suicide.
>
> Those who committed suicide — and there were countless during the Cultural Revolution — were regarded as having 'alienated themselves from the people and the Party.' Overnight, Peiku's life changed. She was called the daughter of a 'dog landlord who had infiltrated teachers' ranks', a 'fake model', and made to attend study sessions where she was investigated and spent endless hours studying Mao's work…

Li had to accept her sacrifice:

> Peiku left without saying goodbye. I found a note waiting for me in my room. 'It's because I love you that I don't want to destroy you.'

Li subsequently married Yinxia on January 6, 1968, but:

> As it happened, two months later, Yinxia's father committed suicide too. He was a country doctor in a commune clinic… but he was denounced as a 'reactionary academic authority.' One night, some rebels

['It is right to rebel', said Mao] placed him in front of a coal-burning stove until he was drenched in sweat, then forced to strip down to his underclothes and sent him outdoors to stand in the snow until he was nearly frozen. The following day he hanged himself.

When I think back to the early 1970s, when there was a vogue for the Cultural Revolution among young western intellectuals, I do not feel amused any longer by their adolescent idiocy: I am angered by it. What was important for them was not the fate of millions but their self-regard. When I see photos of a man bent double for hours in a bow, paraded through the streets of Harbin (Li Fanxi had his hair cut, pulled out and stuffed in his mouth), followed by those of Mao, in his pseudo-proletarian fancy dress smiling and waving contentedly to a crowd of compulsorily — and no doubt hysterically — happy young people in a cinema in the same city when he appears on the screen, I despair of humanity. To this day Mao is untouchable in China because he is the *fons et origo* of all government legitimacy there, much as the Resurrection is to the church.

Cruelty is multiform: it has many pretexts, justifications, reasons and pleasures. Above all, it gratifies those who practise it in the name of a higher good, social, economic, religious, or political. To make others suffer for the good of humanity is a refined, if illicit and seldom acknowledged, pleasure.

My friend in Dublin, Dr Rory O'Donnell, a poet and a man

of refined literary sensibility, gave me on a brief visit to the city a novella by Claire Keegan, which takes as its theme the Magdalen laundries in Ireland, in which unwed mothers were sent to work their penance while their children were adopted away. It is said that up to 30 thousand mothers were sent to them between 1922 and 1996, when they closed. According to most investigators they were the scene of institutionalised cruelty by the nuns who ran them, though the extent of the cruelties practised has been disputed. Of course, Ireland was very poor for much of that period, and it is possible that the distinction between the hardship of poverty and outright cruelty might sometimes have been difficult to make.

When I first went to Ireland, in 1965, the hold of the Catholic church on the population was still limpet-like and the priest in the western counties was a kind of demigod. Every family wanted to have a priest in it as a matter of prestige. Now the revulsion against the church has been complete, and Claire Keegan's novella is a manifestation of it.

Its plot is simple. The protagonist is Bill Furlong, who himself has been born out of wedlock. Fortunately for him and his mother, a widow in a large country house, Mrs Wilson, not coincidentally a Protestant, takes them in and ensures the boy has a sufficient education.[30] When he is old enough, she lends him several thousand pounds to start a business of his own, the delivery of coal and wood to the residents of the small town in which he lives.

In the course of his business, he has large deliveries to make

---

[30] This, of course, is a complete reversal, or mirror-image, of the Catholic-good, Protestant-bad historiography of Ireland.

to the local convent. One day, as he makes a delivery, he discovers a young woman, an unwed mother, locked in the coal cellar. He releases her and takes her back to the main entrance of the convent where the Mother Superior does not admit that it is the nuns who locked her in the cellar, instead blaming the young woman herself for her carelessness.

Bill Furlong is now a conventionally married man with children of his own, whom he wants to give the normal family life that he envied as a child. When he was a boy, he wrote to Santa Claus asking him to bring the father he had never known, though of course this never happened. There is a slight hint that he might be related biologically to a relative of Mrs Wilson's, but there is no certainty in this, and we never discover who the father was, much less meet him.

Bill Furlong tells his wife about the young woman he found in the coal cellar, but she tells him to mind his own business and not to poke his nose into affairs that are none of his business. Although he and his wife are not rich, they are getting by, which is more than many people were able to do at the time (1985). The convent is very powerful in the town, and if he started a scandal about it their business might suffer, and they would be plunged into poverty. The church was still strong to the point of being all-powerful. Attendance at Sunday mass was expected and non-attendance was a social mistake.

Furlong, however, finds the young woman locked in the cellar a second time. Now there can be no doubt as to how she got there. He releases her and takes her home, to brave the wrath of his wife (the story ends before she expresses it). We see a man who has done the right thing no matter the consequences for him personally.

I confess to mixed feelings about the story. It is a powerful denunciation of the Catholic church (and of the state's complicity with it) and of its hold over the population such that people were afraid to speak out against its abuses. In other words, Ireland at the time of the story was an informal totalitarian or theocratic dictatorship in which the grossest abuses and cruelties were ignored though they were there for all to see if they wished, that is to say if they had not blinded themselves to them.

In a matter of a few years, Ireland has gone from poverty to wealth (Dublin is now a bright shining city, albeit that it has lost much of the distinctive atmosphere I remember from more than half a century ago), in which it now requires more courage to defend the Catholic church than to attack it. No good may be said of it, and not a priest or a nun is to be seen on the streets of its capital. In portraying the nuns of the convent as sadists, admittedly more by implication than by literal description, the author is only being deeply conventional (without necessarily being false to history), the plus of the convention having become the minus of an opposite convention, and *vice versa*. I couldn't help feeling that this was an attack on the defenceless, though the defenceless are not necessarily made meritorious by their defencelessness.

Perhaps no defence is possible: that would be the opinion of my friend, Dr O'Donnell, whose anti-Catholicism long pre-dates the present fashion for it and therefore cannot be deemed merely conventional; indeed, in the circumstances in which he grew up, it was quietly courageous. He never believed the doctrine or the dogma, and he saw the unattractive side of priestly power. I respect his views: in a sense they were hard won and the result of observation and experience. I have never lived where priestly power was strong, and I am sure that I would have hated (and sneered at) it.

And yet I cannot help feeling that in repudiating Catholicism so completely, there has been loss for Ireland as well as gain, albeit that I too cannot believe in the doctrine. Besides, although I am insufficiently knowledgeable to say so with authority, I felt that the author of this powerful novella was being unfair if she meant to imply that all nuns ever did in Ireland was lock young mothers in coal cellars and the like. They were nurses and teachers too and did much good as such. It was not that the novella was untrue, it is more that it was not the whole truth, and there is always a temptation to take the part for the whole.

But is it a criticism of a novella that it does not encompass the whole truth? No one can do that, no matter how many hundreds of pages he writes. Is it better to know a partial truth than to know no truth at all?

I should add that I have been an admirer of nuns, at least of the ones I met in Africa. They expected no sublunary reward for their works of charity. They joyfully devoted their lives to the relief of the suffering of very poor people. Whether in the aggregate they made much difference may be doubted, but not their individual goodness.

I remember an Irish nun, then aged 70 (which seemed to me then immensely old), and who must now be long dead, who was responsible — I should say, made herself responsible — for feeding the inmates of a remote prison in Nigeria who would otherwise have starved. I saw her carrying heavy buckets of what to us would be swill but what was manna to the hungry prisoners, some of whom had been awaiting trial for more than ten years and others of whom had been released by judges but had not the money to pay the guards the necessary bribe to let them out as legally required. No one would ever make this nun the protagonist of a novel, however.

Whoever has visited Haiti never loses interest in it. Perhaps no place on earth has so tragic a history or seems so consistently to stagger from disaster to disaster, mainly human but sometimes natural. But even natural disasters in Haiti are multiplied in their doleful effects by human agency — things done or, more usually, not done. The catastrophic earthquake in 2010 that destroyed so much of Port-au-Prince was not stronger than the one that struck Santiago de Chile but caused only four deaths and did little damage. We think of cholera epidemics as natural disasters, but the one that affected Haiti in the same year (the first epidemic of that disease in its entire history) was brought by Nepali troops of the United Nations Peacekeeping Force.

When it comes to human cruelty, it would be hard to beat the system of slavery of the St. Domingue colony, the French half or portion of the island of Hispaniola, as Haiti was called before the Haitian Revolution. No doubt it is accounted for by the common view among the planters that the slaves were scarcely human at all, more beasts of burden, to be flogged into productivity. It is therefore surprising that two of the great liberators of the Revolution, Toussaint Louverture and Jean-Jacques Dessalines fought initially for the French army, no doubt believing in the protestations of universal brotherhood of the French Revolution. Dessalines ended (that is, before his own assassination) in committing genocide against the French, including small children. It might have been understandable, but it was still genocide, and I suppose Dessalines must be the only genocidal leader who has been commemorated both on banknotes and postage stamps long after his death.

I have an interesting article extracted from *The Penny Magazine*, a publication of the Society for the Diffusion of Useful Knowledge, dated 1838 and titled *Account of Toussain L'Ouverture*.

The Penny Magazine ran from 1832 to 1845, being the brainchild of Whig politicians who wanted to educate the lower orders rather than keep them in ignorance: it was a project that Boris Johnson would no doubt have called 'levelling up'.

At least initially, the magazine was an enormous success. It had a circulation of 200,000, the equivalent today in Britain of about 1.6 million, and would have been read by many more. It was aimed at people with little formal education, but it was written without condescension and assumed a power of concentration on the part of its readers that some university students might now find difficult to equal, at least if reports are to be believed.

One of the reasons for *The Penny Magazine*'s success, apart from its readers' great thirst for knowledge, whether useful or not, and which was probably desired for its own sake, was that it was illustrated, though often with illustrations of doubtful accuracy. The picture of Toussaint L'Ouverture, for example, accompanying the article, is a rather crude adaptation of a portrait found in Marcus Rainsford's *An Historical Account of the Black Empire of Hayti*, published in 1805. Rainsford was a British officer of Irish origin who was for a time a prisoner in Haiti during the Revolution, and who was sentenced to death but reprieved and set free. But the picture in Rainsford's book is itself crude and clearly not drawn from the life. It is of a generic European with a black complexion.

The Whigs were opponents both of the slave trade and of slavery itself, and the *Account of Toussain L'Ouverture* can be taken as a refutation of a common justification of both. The article begins:

> It is an important question whether negroes are constitutionally and therefore irredeemably inferior to whites in the powers of the mind.

The importance of this question is self-evident to the writer, for it bears on 'the vast population of Africa' (which, incidentally, seems destined to make up a larger proportion of the human race than in the past) and of 'some millions of negroes who live elsewhere.' The article continues:

> Many persons have ventured upon peremptory answers on both sides of the question but the majority are still unsatisfied as to the real capacities of the negro race. Their actual [i.e. present] inferiority of mind is too evident to be disputed; but it may be accounted for the circumstances amidst which the negroes have lived, both

in their own countries and abroad; while, if one single instance can be adduced of a man of jet-black complexion who has exhibited a genius which would be considered eminent in civilized European society, we have at least a proof that there is not incompatibility between negro organization and high intellectual power.

This account of Toussaint L'Ouverture then answers the question unequivocally in the affirmative. It is highly admirative, if not hagiographical, of the man. He combines great ability and intelligence with high moral qualities, always dealing justly with others of whatever race, and free of the hatred or resentment which would have been all too understandable in the circumstances. In the end it was his attachment to honour that undid him and was his downfall, and his naïve faith in the honour of those with whom he had to deal. He was taken prisoner by the French with whom he was negotiating, removed to France, imprisoned in abominable conditions, and died soon afterwards. The article ends:

> Was this not a man? — in all respects worthy of the name? He was altogether African — a perfect negro in his organization, yet a fully endowed and well-accomplished man. In no respect does his nature to have been deemed unequal; there is no feebleness in one direction as a consequence of unusual vigour in another. He had strength of body, strength of understanding, strength of belief, and consequently of purpose; strength of affection, of imagination, and of will. He was

emphatically a great Man: and what one man of his race
has been, others may be.

The whole article is implicitly an attack on the idea that it is
morally permissible to enslave negroes because they are by
constitution inferior intellectually, and therefore to treat them
as lower than children in capacity or rights. Strictly speaking
it would not follow that if their IQ were lower on average than
that of another race that it would be ethically justified to inflict
upon them the kind of horrors that were actually inflicted
upon them, or even to treat its individuals in any way
differently from individuals of another race. After all, the
normal distributions of intelligence of two human races
overwhelmingly overlap. The Dutch are the tallest people in
the world, but you could not conclude from this that an
individual Dutchman must be taller than any individual of any
other nation.

At any rate, I think it can be seen from the passages that I
have quoted that the writers of *The Penny Magazine* presumed
a high level of literacy in their readers: higher than that of, say,
the readers of the *Daily Telegraph* today.

I like to think that, unlike the rest of humanity, I am not
unduly susceptible to suggestion by advertisement. Partly this
is because there is very little that I buy, apart from books.
When I come to think of it, however, I often buy books
because of reviews of them that I have read, and perhaps this
is often not so very distant from advertising. The literary

editors of publications are, after all, lobbied by the publicity departments of publishing firms, and all kinds of considerations other than the purest literary merit affect decisions about which books to review. Besides, literary editors behave like a flock of sheep: they always have an eye on what their competitors and confreres are doing, and wish to do likewise. And I have heard more than one literary editor say that, though perfectly aware that a certain book is not worth a review, he or she has to 'do' it because such-and-such a publication has reviewed it, or that it has been reviewed everywhere, and to stand out negatively would for some reason be too risky. Perhaps this helps to explain a little the tendency of people to go along with totalitarian governments. If people are afraid not to conform even in conditions of perfect safety, is it hardly any wonder that they conform when there are real reasons to fear?

I read reviews of a book by Simon Parkin about Nikolai Vavilov's seed bank in what was then called Leningrad, which was the largest such bank in the world, and which the staff of the Plant Institute which held it refused to eat even while they were starving to death during the Nazi siege of the city that lasted three years. The story is interwoven with that of Vavilov himself, a plant geneticist who fell foul of Stalin on ideological grounds, not believing, as was then obligatory, in the heritability of acquired characteristics and that the environment therefore accounted for all biological variation, at least within species such as wheat and *Homo sapiens*.

Vavilov was a world-famous scientist — famed, that is, in scientific circles — but his fame, far from protecting him from Stalin's paranoid wrath, made him of all men the most suspect, practically an enemy agent. He was arrested, tortured, and mistreated to death in prison in Saratov, the city in southern Russia (a thousand miles from Petersburg) where, years before, he had been a professor, and where he now starved to death.

I bought the book at St Pancras Station on my way to Paris. It was an ill-fated volume. As I climbed into the carriage of the train with it under my arm as I tried also to lift a heavy suitcase, it slipped and fell between the carriage and the track. I would have left it there, but my wife was determined to retrieve it. She found a railway employee who, as it happened, was equipped for just such an eventuality or emergency. He had a kind of pincer precisely for this situation, which was evidently common enough, and he retrieved the book which was, surprisingly, very little damaged by its adventure.

The next day, I took it with me on the Paris Métro, having only a very few pages left to read. The train broke down at the station of the Place de la République, at a time when the carriage made a tin of sardines seem like a *fête champêtre*. Everyone complained but no one behaved badly. After about fifteen minutes, however, we were all told to alight. I decided to walk to my destination, a mile and a half away. Before I set out, I sat on a bench in the Place to phone my wife to tell her what I was doing. Then I set out and after a few hundred yards realised that I had left the book behind on the bench. I returned, but not surprisingly for so frequented a place, it had gone.

Once again, my wife came to my rescue. She ordered the book on the internet, and I had it the next day. But still it struck me as odd that a particular copy of a book should have been so ill-fated. Freud, with his belief that one never does anything by accident, might have made something of my dropping and then leaving it.

In view of the subject matter of the book, I was a little ashamed at the depth of my despair on each occasion when I thought I had lost it. Despair, for such a trifling cause!

A question in the book that the author raises — perhaps because there is no definitive answer to it — is whether the extreme heroism of the staff of the Institute was either justified or reasonable. At all costs they wanted to preserve the collection and preferred to die than to eat it. One of the survivors, asked many years later the question whether the sacrifice had been worth it, replied:

Imagine the scenario: here you are — a writer, who has written a book. You've put your all into it: your whole life. And suddenly, let's say, there is a severe frost, and you find yourself in a room without firewood to keep warm, only your manuscript... Now can you begin to understand the psychology of the situation? You are freezing to death: will you destroy this, the only copy of your book? Would you die to preserve your book? Yes, or no? Will you give in to temptation? What are you asking me: you and all the others? You're surprised? You're perplexed? Yes, it was difficult to walk at that time. It was unbearably difficult to get up every morning, move your hands and feet... But to refrain from eating the collection? That wasn't difficult. No, not at all, because it was impossible to eat your life's work, the life's work of your friends and colleagues. Do I really need to prove such elementary, simple things to you?

Ask yourself this: is there anything in your life for which you would do likewise, and if not, have you in some sense wasted it?

Vavilov was by all accounts a remarkable and almost wholly admirable man, brilliant without arrogance, and very cultivated. He was an elegant dresser at a time when to dress well was probably dangerous and certainly a triumph of the human spirit. He was polyglot and Anglophile when there was still something to be *philic* about. He was no armchair scientist: he led expeditions to the remotest parts of the globe to collect seeds that he could cross with seeds already known, to yield crops that might help obviate the risk of famine or hunger — surely a noble goal? At any rate, he dedicated his whole life to it.

One reads of how such a man was treated with absolute horror. He was tortured to confess to imaginary crimes, the torturer himself afraid of being tortured if he did not extract a confession, though he knew the crimes never to have been committed. (I once had a Syrian patient whose profession in the army had been torturer until he was arrested, imprisoned and tortured in turn, using the very methods he had employed. Or so he said.) The starving and dying Vavilov asked the prison governor for some rice water, a modest request that outraged and infuriated the governor. The request was refused, and Vavilov died two days later of hunger. The post-mortem report — they performed them! — said, 'Subcutaneous cellular tissue absent.'

When I wrote 'how such a man was treated,' I suddenly had

a shock. Was it because he was such a man that his torture was so abominable? Would it have been better, or not so bad, if he had been a man of no particular accomplishment, for example not a foreign Fellow of the Royal Society?

I am reminded of the ghastly victim impact statements now allowed at murder trials after a guilty verdict. A close relative of the murdered person extols him or her: such a lovely smile, so good at football, etc. But is this not all beside the point, namely that a life has been wrongly and feloniously taken away?

Of what use are old medical textbooks? The methods they describe are obsolete, their therapeutics likewise, and perhaps even their nosology (their classification of diseases) has been overtaken by new knowledge. They are bulky and heavy: indeed, the very idea of a medical textbook is now obsolete. All necessary information is available online and updated daily by electronic means. To have stopped practising even a short time ago is to have become out-of-date. The pace of medical advance — or at any rate change — is impressive, but for old doctors there is an edge of melancholy to it. Who wants to be a fossil before his time?

But old medical textbooks are of historical interest. My copy of W. Russell Brain's *Diseases of the Nervous System*, the fourth edition, dates from 1951. The preface to the third edition, published in 1947, says, 'Owing to the war seven years have passed since the last edition of this book was published. Modern war always improves medical knowledge... The war has thrown new light upon the nature of peripheral nerve injuries and placed their classification and treatment on a sounder basis. Conditions prevailing in prisoner-of-war camps have, unhappily, provided the opportunity of studying deficiency diseases on a larger scale than ever before...' This is one way of putting it. Medical knowledge so dearly bought takes many years, centuries, to pay off its mortgage, so to speak, if it can ever do so.

My copy of this textbook once belonged to my predecessor in my last post. It bears his dated signature — September 1951. I am tempted to add, 73 years ago already! He was, I am told, a clever and kind man, but he was an alcoholic, and it was this that destroyed him. When I took over from him, I discovered quarter bottles of vodka secreted everywhere he had an office, like Stations of the Cross. He died not very long after his forced retirement, much lamented by everyone who knew him, except perhaps his divorced and long-suffering wife.

Medical knowledge can be effectively lost as well as gained, though of course the loss is miniscule by comparison with the gain, more particularly when a disease has been all but eliminated. This is the case with General Paralysis of the Insane (GPI), the last stage of tertiary syphilis. It vanished with the advent of penicillin but must at one time have furnished many a patient for the lunatic asylum.

I once wrote a short article in the *British Medical Journal* about Henrik Ibsen's play, *Ghosts*. The question was whether it was possible for hereditary (actually, congenital) syphilis to pass to offspring via the father alone, and also whether it could manifest itself for the first time, as it did in the play, as mental deterioration in the sufferer's early twenties. I asked several venereologists, but they did not know, their experience of the disease having been now so limited. I sought out Alfred Fournier's book *La Syphilis héréditaire tardive* (Late Hereditary Syphilis), but being far from a library, and the only copies for sale that I could find costing hundreds of pounds, I almost gave up. But looking on eBay for the first time in my life, I found a copy for sale not only with a dedication by the great French syphilologist, but at only £5, the first book to be advertised on the screen when I looked. As Kafka would have put it, someone must have been following my searches on the internet...

Ibsen was right, though at the time the evidence could only very recently have been discovered. It is said that after the age of 50, Ibsen read only the newspapers and the Bible, though perhaps medical journals as well.

I looked up GPI in Brain's textbook of neurology because I thought that Nietzsche must have suffered from it (Thomas Mann had no doubts on the matter). If he, Nietzsche, had it, it surely accounts for some of his bombast:

> The earliest symptoms are usually mental, and in the early stages they are frequently so slight as to be apparent only to those who know the patient well... The form taken by the mental disorder... doubtless depends on the patient's mental constitution... The grandiose form... is less common than simple dementia. Patients of this [grandiose] type are euphoric and develop delusions in which they figure as exceptional persons endowed with superhuman strength, immense wealth, or other

magnificent attributes... and they see no discrepancy between their imaginary attributes and their debilitated and unfortunate actual condition... As the patient becomes worse... the symptoms of dementia become more prominent, and in the terminal stages there is little evidence of any mental activity, and the sufferer, bedridden, incoherent and dirty, leads a vegetative existence.

This seems to fit Nietzsche pretty well (there are always variations in clinical presentations), and the terrible headaches from which he suffered may well have been a symptom of meningovascular syphilis.

One of the lessons one might draw from this textbook of neurology, which ran through several more editions, is that there has been a great change in our sensibility since. Throughout the book are interspersed pictures of patients without any attempt to hide or disguise their identity. Those who knew them would have recognised them at once and have been able to name them. Such medical insensitivity or exercise of power would be unthinkable today, and one cannot help but ask whether the patients whose photographs were used in the textbook had been asked for their permission. If they were, perhaps they were told that their permission would assist medical science, and if so, indignity would have been changed into something noble, of which to be proud rather than ashamed.

Another thing noticeable in old textbooks is the extremity of the pathology illustrated, almost never seen today. For example, the picture shown of exophthalmic ophthalmoplegia would be all but impossible to provide today, for no case would have progressed so far. There are many things that are unattractive about the modern world, but not the absence of the grossest pathology.

Brain touches upon the psychological aspects of neurology: after all, it is still the case that about half of patients who attend neurology clinics have no detectable neurological lesion. The explanation given for hysterical paralysis and the like could hardly be bettered:

> The purpose served by the symptoms can usually be expressed as the unconscious solution, however unsatisfactory, of a mental conflict. The patient finds himself in a situation in which a course of action which he desires to follow conflicts with his sense of duty or of self-respect. The development of the hysterical symptom unconsciously solves the conflict, though at the cost of a neurotic disability. For example, a girl was compelled to give up her work to look after her invalid mother. She developed an hysterical paralysis of her right hand which prevented her from doing housework, and assistance had to be obtained to look after both her mother and herself. Her hysterical illness saved her from the unpleasant duty and also preserved her self-respect since she felt that no one could blame her for being ill. At the same time, she ceased to do any work at all, unconsciously revenged herself on her exacting parent, and became an object of sympathy to those with whom she came in contact.

This is much better than Freud: and in fact, fifty years after the book was published, I had precisely such a patient. She developed an hysterical paralysis of her leg which rendered her incapable of looking after her husband, never much loved by her, after he became a cardiac invalid following a heart attack at the time of his retirement. She required care herself, and her family insisted that there was something physically wrong with her because they did not want to admit that their family had ever been less than perfectly happy. Removed physically from the situation, however, she swiftly recovered the use of her leg, which because useless again whenever she returned home.

Next to my Brain, as it were, is ranged on my bookshelf a very slim volume indeed, titled *De l'Ennui*, Of Boredom, by A. Briere de Boismont. How I came by this 41-page essay, published in 1850, I do not know, but I do remember that I had it bound in cloth by a second-hand bookseller who was learning book-binding. He was a communist of the Enver Hoxha faction, believing Albania to be the nearest to heaven on earth that the latter could offer. He had a kind of evangelical zeal for the memoirs of Hoxha, which he always tried to sell to respectable black ladies who were in search of a Bible, not with any success even according to him. I doubt that Hoxha's fulminations against the Tito-ites and the Khrushchev-ites would have meant much to them anyway; anyone who was known to the bookseller by the suffix *-ite* was a kind of heretic or traitor, as the Mutazilites were heretics to the Moslems. He sold very good books very cheaply, however, in an area of the city where you would least have expected it. What became of him I do not know; he refused to move with the times, for example by installing the internet which he regarded as a capitalist tool to stupefy the masses who would otherwise have followed the Albanian path to socialism. That the internet could stupefy was undeniable, but I doubt that, were it not for the stupefaction it promoted, the world would have imitated Albania under Hoxha. I got on very well with the bookseller.

Alexandre Briere de Boismont (1797–1881) was a French alienist, or mad-doctor, who write on a wide range of subjects, but whose most famous work was *Hallucinations, or the Rational History of Apparitions, Visions, Dreams, Ecstasy, Magnetism, and Somnambulism*. He was the founder-editor of the *Annales Médico-psychologiques*, from which *De l'Ennui* was an extract.

Nineteenth century alienists wrote very well, with fine descriptions of their patients, perhaps because there was little else they could do but describe them, as often is still the case today, the difference with the alienists of today being their prose style. Now, however, psychiatrists fear to be thought mere litterateurs rather than real scientists, so their prose has become indigestible, the indispensable first stage of seriousness.

Boismont's essay begins well:

> The man who thinks is an animal depraved, a famous philosopher wrote somewhere: it would have been more natural to say an animal bored.

It is true that boredom is a much-underestimated factor in

human psychology, and perhaps in human history. When people pray for universal peace, I can't help thinking, 'How boring it would be!' I should add that I am by no means bellicose or belligerent; but one cannot help but notice that descriptions of heaven are boring by comparisons with those of hell.

Boismont continues:

> My paper, *The Influence of civilisation on the development of madness* was much criticised when I read it twelve years ago at the Institute.[31] If I published it today, would anyone believe that events since then were of a nature to modify my conclusions? Well, what I asserted then about the prevalence of madness in civilised countries I can now assert about boredom with even more reason.

But the boredom of which Boismont speaks is not that temporary state of emptiness the person feels when the amusements or distractions, real or virtual, that play an ever greater role in our lives cease and which can be alleviated by a resumption of such distractions as usual. He speaks rather of the *taedium vitae* of the Hamlet variety, the kind that makes the Prince exclaim, 'How weary, stale, flat and unprofitable seems to me all the uses of this world.' It is not so much the absence of interest at this moment of which our author writes, but of the feeling that human existence itself is intrinsically boring because there is no point to it. Of course, this *taedium vitae* might itself be fleeting: I feel something of it when I am

---

[31] *L'Institut de France.*

confronted by a boring bureaucratic task that is time-consuming and difficult of accomplishment, but which strikes me as pointless. It casts a gloom, temporarily, over the whole of existence, though it lifts as soon as the task is completed. But there are some people who feel this gloom the whole of their lives, or at least for much of them.

Boismont describes the melancholic temperament which can predominate over any good fortune and conduce to suicide:

> A young man of twenty-five, highly placed in point of fortune, living in the midst of a family, loved by all, had been, since his childhood, of a sad temperament. The passing years did not change it; he was habitually sombre and melancholic, and when anyone asked his reasons for his taciturnity, he avoided explanations... He seldom joined in the amusements of his friends... He was always cold, reserved and untrusting. Three weeks ago, he was seen making the wooden planks that would serve as preparations for his death; questioned on the use to which he wanted to put them, he confined himself to saying that we would see later.

The planks were to protect the floor from being stained by his blood when he shot himself. He wrote that it was already too much that his father's house should be the scene of his death; he did not want it physically stained as well. Before his suicide, he wrote to the painter who had just painted his portrait:

> By the time you receive this letter, I will live only in the

picture that you have executed so well. My eyes will be extinguished, and only this image will be able to remind my poor father of what they once were.

Briere de Boismont had studied suicide notes.

> One finds in the words, the writing, of those who kill themselves, their character, their habits, their mode of life, even the influences that led them to do what they have done. Some are tired of life because it is humiliating to serve people; yet others leave without saying goodbye because they have no one to say it to... "Punishments, privations, obedience!" cried a soldier, "I want no more of them. Let them gather up my body and bury it; that's the only favour I ask for. I have never thought of God, and I don't believe in another life."

I once discovered that those who make superficially suicidal gestures in the full knowledge that they would not die left suicide notes as frequently as those who actually killed themselves, contrary to the generally accepted doctrine on this matter. I asked myself whether it would be possible to distinguish the degree of true suicidality by the content of the notes. (I recall one adolescent who wrote, 'Goodbye mum and dad. I guess I have a lot of growing up to do.') In my experience, the notes of those who succeed in putting an end to their days were short and to the point: 'I can't take any more,' 'I've had enough,' 'Sorry.'

But was my impression correct? I sent a junior doctor to the coroner's office to find the suicide notes preserved there. The archives, it turned out, were a complete mess: here the electric fire with which L….. S…. electrocuted himself in the bath, there the rope with which C….. B….. hanged himself, there again the knife with which R….. G….. cut his throat, and there the bottle of bleach that M… F…… drank. It was impossible to complete the study, and I moved on to other subjects, equally depressing.

My brother-in-law, like me, is a great reader, though unlike me he does other things as well. He is particularly a reader of history, and among the books he brought with him on a recent stay in our house in France was *L'Inquisition espagnole* by Bartolomé Bennassar, published in 1979. He bought it second-hand for next to nothing, attracted by the hand-written inscription on the inside of the front cover:

> *Maurice, Ne passe plus jamais les vacances sur la Costa del Sol —*
> *sous chaque pierre un juif dort. A.H. – Y.A. dec 1983.*
> Maurice, never again spend your holidays on the Costa del Sol — under every stone there sleeps a Jew. A.H. – Y.A. December, 1983.

My brother-in-law thought the inscription was from one Jewish person to another, but I suggested that it might have been from one fanatic antisemite to another, warning him of the danger of vengeful Jewish spirits, or even physical pollution, everywhere. The former interpretation was far the more likely, of course, but words do not always speak for themselves and are open to differing interpretations.

As, of course, are historical events and movements themselves, including the Spanish Inquisition, in the case of the latter no interpretation being definitive. Inspired by my brother-in-law, I re-read a book by the pre-eminent British historian of the Inquisition, Henry Kamen, *Inquisition and Society in Spain in the Sixteenth and Seventeenth Centuries*. Published in 1985, it was itself a revision of another he wrote in 1965 (the author, born in 1938, is still living). Whether or how far the historiography of the Inquisition has moved on since 1985, I cannot say. On the vast majority of the subjects about which you read, you are at the mercy of the last thing your read, and the latest might not be the best.

When I say that Kamen's book seems to me morally confused, I do not mean it as a criticism: it is indeed difficult or impossible to pass indubitable and final judgments on the distant, or even the recent, past. By what standards are the actors in distantly past events to be judged? By our own contemporary ones, which — though we may disclaim it — we believe to be a full and final state of enlightenment? In the case of the Spanish Inquisition, is it by sixteenth, seventeenth, eighteenth or even nineteenth century standards that we should judge it? (It was founded in 1480 and abolished once and for all in 1824.) Is it to be judged by Castilian or Aragonese standards (the two kingdoms were joined by marriage and were very different), or by world standards, if any such monster exists? And this is quite apart from the fact that two historians, writing at the same time and in the same country, about the same facts (more or less), may come to very different moral conclusions. I should add, perhaps, that there may also be disputes as to what the facts actually were: they do not stand still like the megaliths of Stonehenge.

It is not surprising, then, that a conscientious historian like Kamen sounds now like a defender, now like a prosecutor, of the Spanish Inquisition. It is one of those subjects about which it is difficult to sound, let alone be, neutral, even when one seems to change one's mind within the space of a couple of paragraphs.

On the defence side, Kamen tells us that the Inquisition set its face against accusations of witchcraft, not by denying the possibility or existence of witchcraft, but by scrupulously demanding evidence that it had been employed — which demand, of course, could never be met. This is not without historical importance, because in other parts of Europe tens, perhaps hundreds, of thousands of women — the old, the mad, and the ugly, as well as the hysterical, to say nothing of those who simply aroused the enmity of someone or other — were killed as witches. It is in large part thanks to the Spanish Inquisition that Spain escaped the witchcraft craze.

The supposedly frightful prisons of the Inquisition, says Kamen, were in reality a good deal less revolting than those of the civil authorities. Indeed, they were almost comfortable by comparison.

Then, of course, there is the question of numbers. There is no denying that in the first two decades of its operation, the Inquisition brought about a kind of holocaust. But Ferdinand and Isabella were not antisemitic as such (at least, not according to Kamen). The object of the expulsion of the Jews from Spain was not racial: it was to remove the temptation of the *conversos*, the Jews who had converted to Catholicism, that it to say half the original Jewish population of the peninsula, to revert to their original religion. But once the Jews who had refused to convert and who did not disguise their Judeity had emigrated — to Portugal, to Venice, to Turkey — there was the suspicion, which according to Kamen was not unjustified in all cases, that many of the *conversos*, or New Christians, were secret Judaizers, that is to say people who conformed outwardly and publicly to Catholic rites but returned to Jewish beliefs and rites in their homes. And it was the richer part of the Jewish population that had, nominally at least, converted, and was afterwards prominent in trade, banking, law, medicine, administration and even the Church. As in every society, a successful minority excited the resentment of the less successful, so that at first the Inquisition, which concentrated its attention on those people who were most resented, was popular, or at least not unpopular. Torquemada, the first and most notorious of the Grand Inquisitors, was himself of partly Jewish extraction.

Once the first paroxysm was over, the Inquisition, having supposedly eliminated the Judaizers, sought enemies to extirpate (few organisations dissolve themselves once their mission has been accomplished, and so find other missions to accomplish). The Inquisition in effect prevented the spread of Protestantism in Spain, and there were no wars of religion in Spain as there were in France and Germany, in which, respectively, three million and a third of the population died. Thus, the Inquisition had the effect, if not the intention, of saving perhaps millions of Spanish lives, albeit at a cost of imposing a religious uniformity that we now abominate.

The Inquisition, says Kamen, did not affect the majority of

Spaniards in the slightest, not least because its means were so limited. Nor was it avaricious: it accumulated no wealth. The effect of its censorship was almost nil: not only did the golden age of Spanish literature coincide with its active stage, but not a single work of science ever fell under its prohibition. This is contrary to what all people who grew up in Protestant countries were taught and mostly believe (that is, when they were taught anything at all). Finally, its methods were less rather than more cruel than those of other tribunals of their time, and not only in Spain.

Against this, there is also no doubt that, especially in the towns, the Inquisition inspired terror. The accused were not told who their accuser was, nor of what they were accused, until they were confronted with it in court (they never learned who their accusers were). Anything that could identify the accuser, such as place or date, was removed from the accusation, so that defence was rendered impossible. The trial became a game of blind man's bluff, with severe punishment at the end: loss of name, loss of possessions, loss of livelihood and sometimes loss of life. This was a third Kafka, a third NKVD, and a third Cultural Revolution. It was not so much mediaeval as modern: and if reports are to be believed, something resembling the Spanish Inquisition has been set up in many institutions, especially universities. Apart from anything else, inquisitions are *fun* — for those which are on the inquisitorial side, that is.

Among the most ferocious defenders of the Spanish

Inquisition was Joseph de Maistre, the Savoyard political philosopher who was Sardinian ambassador to St Petersburg for several years. His *Lettres à un gentilhomme russe sur l'Inquisition espagnole* (Letters to a Russian Gentleman on the Spanish Inquisition) were edited by his son Rodolphe and published in 1822, a year after Maistre's death. The letters are well worth reading and no one could accuse Maistre of having been mealy mouthed.

My copy was awarded as a second prize for excellence in his philosophy class to one Louis de Sucy on the 18th April 1835. The institution in which the latter was a pupil or student is not mentioned specifically, but it was presided over by a *Prêtre supérieur* of the name of Poiloup, who ran a school in the rue Vaugirard in Paris, where, four years after the award of the prize to Louis de Sucy, the great painter, Édouard Manet, was to be a pupil.

Maistre says much the same as does Kamen, more than a century and a half in advance. Maistre makes much of the relative tranquillity of Spain by comparison with France, Germany and England in the sixteenth and seventeenth centuries, and attributes this difference entirely to the operation of the Spanish Inquisition in enforcing religious uniformity. No doubt, had he been alive today, he would have taken malicious delight in our doctrinally uniform belief in the glories of doctrinal diversity.

Maistre was a believing Catholic, but his arguments in the *Lettres* do not touch on the truth (or otherwise) of Catholic doctrine. His first argument is that enforcement of it in Spain saved many lives, and his second argument is that those who attacked the Inquisition as detestable were themselves detestable hypocrites.

He reserved his particular odium — and he had great reserves of it — for the English, who claimed (at the time he was writing) to be religiously tolerant but whose history was replete with violent intolerance which he attributed to Protestantism, a religion which remembered persecutions suffered but never persecutions inflicted.

No one could say that Maistre wrote with judicial impartiality. When he deals with the Inquisition's comparative mildness, he attributes it to the clerical nature of the institution, but when he deals with its excesses (which he admits occurred), he attributes them to the fact that it was, at root, an arm of the state and not of the Church. But Maistre was not the first, and was certainly not the last, whose conclusions determined the argument rather than the other way round. He being a brilliant polemicist, however, one does not realise what he is doing while he is doing it until one pauses to reflect. And such is the quality of Maistre's prose that he drives one on without such pause.

When it comes to the vaunted religious tolerance of the English (although the Catholic Emancipation Act was still a few years off), Maistre characterises it as religious indifference, that is to say an absence of real, living belief. For him, a real believer in the truth of his religion must want to impose it upon others. After all, if it is true that only by believing x can you enter the Kingdom of Heaven and avoid Hell, you are doing your fellow-creature no favour by not impelling him to believe x. And the only way to do this is to indoctrinate him from an early age. This in turn means that as tight as possible a control must be held over society, especially in the realm of thought.

Once granted the premise, there is logic to the system, but Maistre does not examine the premise. To do so would be the beginning of inevitable decay: and after all, every society must be founded upon some basic premise, even if it is not consciously acknowledged. You have to start from (or is it stop?) somewhere, that somewhere being not itself a matter of rational choice, but of faith. And — according to Maistre — Catholicism has proved its superiority as a faith, not least in the social peace it brought about by comparatively mild means, to say nothing of the beauties that the faith has inspired.

Tolerance for Maistre is nothing but infidelity, which is for him both despicable and dangerous, and needful to be suppressed. He cites a lady who writes to an Anglican prelate, asking him whether the fact that her daughter wished to marry a man of a different religious persuasion or sect should affect her relations with her. The prelate replies that so long as the proposed son-in-law is a man of good character and adheres to the basic tenets of Christianity, she should accept him wholeheartedly. Most of us would think that this was rather decent of the prelate[32], but for Maistre this only goes to show that the prelate doesn't really believe anything much. How could a church survive such broadmindedness? It could dispense with itself altogether. For Maistre, religious belief was all or nothing. If he had been born in a Moslem country, he would undoubtedly have been a Wahhabi.

Maistre turns his vituperation particularly on England

---

[32] The decency would, of course, depend on what counted as the basic tenets to which the prelate was referring.

because, he says, it is undoubtedly the most important and successful Protestant country:

> You will perhaps say the convulsions in England have ceased; its present condition has cost it streams of blood, but in the end this country has been raised to such a height of grandeur to excite the envy of other nations.

To this, Maistre has an answer:

> I reply first that no one is obliged to buy future happiness at the expense of the present miseries; the sovereign who makes such a calculation is both foolhardy and culpable. Therefore, the Kings of Spain who, by very little blood of the impure, stop the torrents of blood… made an excellent calculation and remain irreproachable.

Of all the figures that Maistre detests (Maistre, though a clubbable man in person and social life, was a first-class hater in print), David Hume stands first. He recognises him, correctly in my view, as the most dangerous enemy intellectually, and therefore in the last resort practically as well, of religion. He is particularly horrified by Hume's apparent levity and calmness on his deathbed. If a man does not repent his irreligion on his own deathbed, he is irreligious indeed. He recognises Hume as incomparably the intellectual superior of Voltaire, which made him all the more dangerous. Where Voltaire sniggered, Hume reasoned. Hume was a true atheist, and for Maistre that was enough reason to abominate him. He was, so to speak, the logical conclusion of English

Protestantism.

At no point, however, does Maistre try to refute Hume. An undesirable, or undesired, consequence of a chain of reasoning is for Maistre sufficient reason to reject it. This is by no means an uncommon way to argue, and I may indeed sometimes have done so myself.

The subject of cults and religious sects once came up for me this way: we had invited a young man who helps us in our garden in France to lunch, when he discovered that my wife now makes our own bread, bags of flour, bowls of dough, and baking tins being much in evidence. He remarked that making one's own bread had become something of a cult, and from this remark it was an easy step to talking about the Aum Supreme Truth sect that in 1995 released sarin gas in the Tokyo underground railway system, killing several passengers and laying low thousands (we couldn't remember how many, exactly).

Our gardener was a boy at the time, but we — my wife and I — were then middle-aged. We remembered something about a mad guru, but the details escaped us, so much water having flowed under our bridges since.

However, I did remember that I bought a book about it soon afterwards, which I had always intended to read but had somehow omitted to do so. I had it still in my library, and it so happened that it was in that fifth of the library that I had catalogued, and I was therefore able to find it with ease.

Though I buy more books than I can read, I never buy a

book that I do not intend to read, and sometimes, as in this case, I read it twenty-eight years after having bought it.

The title of the book was *The Cult at the End of the World: The Incredible Story of Aum*. It was by two journalists, David E. Kaplan and Andrew Marshall. It would be difficult to make a dull book of such a subject, and in fact I read it straight through, appalled but fascinated. Assuming the authors to be honest, which I took them to be, I found the book to be of admirable thoroughness.

The story would be scarcely credible were not Mankind so capable of such absurdity as belief in something as silly as Aum combined with high levels of intelligence. 'Readers,' say the authors at the beginning of their short prefatory note, 'may find portions of the book difficult to believe.' If so, they will never have such difficulties believing anything about human possibilities again.

Shoko Asahara, whose real name was Chizuo Matsumoto, was born into a poor family in Southern Japan in 1955, blind in one eye and with very poor vision in the other. A bully and petty swindler in his school for the blind, he worked his way up (if *up* is the direction to describe it) to being the head of a cult which had as its philosophy a kind of spiritual Mickey Finn, drawing from Buddhism, Hinduism and Christianity, laced with absurd eschatology. Its doctrine was kaleidoscopic in its changes, but it attracted large numbers of devotees, not only in Japan, but especially in Russia, and not only those of feeble intellect, but mathematicians, astrophysicists, geneticists, chemists, and so forth. The guru himself was not the intellectual equal of these clever but warped followers, but somehow he managed to dominate them until they were subordinate. If the book teaches nothing else, it teaches that intellectual brilliance is no defence — not necessarily a defence, that is — against idiocy, and may even be idiocy's staunchest ally, insofar as a brilliant mind once possessed of idiocy knows best how to defend it and make it seem clear and obvious to others. An intelligent madman is more dangerous than a stupid one.

Because the doctrine of the sect, which was able to run closed communities, was so unstable, though always apocalyptic, it is difficult to summarise it. The golden thread of paranoia that ran through it was that the end was nigh, except for those who were faithful to Shoko Asahara. As with other such sects, adherents abandoned everything to join it — their families, their jobs, their friends — and donated all their worldly goods to it. They were soon trapped and could not leave even when they suffered continual abuse. Most of those who joined were vulnerable in some way, even if it was only that they were in search of some transcendent meaning in their life that was otherwise mundane.

I saw such sects at work a few times in the course of my career. A young man — it was usually, though not always, a young man — who lived on the streets because of his drug addiction would be netted, so to speak, by a Christian sect that would offer him home, food, support, etc., and free him of his drug-taking. Compared with the disdain or distaste with which almost everyone else regarded him, the members of the sect treated him with what seemed at first regard and lovingkindness, and for a time he felt constrained to believe, and perhaps for a time really *did* believe, in its religious doctrine. Once free of drugs, he would be set to work, at no wages but for his keep alone, in one of the sect's commercial enterprises. Having been cut off from all other sources of social contact and possessed neither of money nor of the right to social security, and his identity papers, if he ever had any, having been removed from him, he had little choice other than to go back on to the streets than to stay within the confines of the sect.

But Aum Supreme Truth, under its bizarre and grotesque guru, took the technique to an altogether higher or more extreme plane. It killed dissenters and then turned them into unrecognisably charred remains. It imprisoned and tortured with impunity in the midst of a modern society under the very eyes of the police. It kidnapped and killed those whom it feared might expose the truth about it. But more amazing still, it recruited scientists who were willing and able to develop on its behalf weapons of mass destruction — chemical and biological — on a scale that would previously have been possible only for a state. It simultaneously boasted of what it was doing, denied it and accused others of what it was doing itself, in particular the Japanese and American governments. In its mad and incoherent way, it thought that the apocalypse it wanted to bring about was inevitable anyway and wanted to get in first. The sarin attack in Tokyo was but the first step in this apocalypse.

Sarin is not easy to produce, and it requires knowledge, determination and skill to do so: in short high intelligence and technical competence. The intelligence was completely disconnected from any minimally rational end. On the contrary, the end was so crazy that it supposedly justified any quantity of mayhem and cruelty.[33] The gas attack which luckily killed only five could have killed thousands and was intended to do so.

The story in the book ends before Asahara and six others were sentenced to death. In fact, they were executed by hanging only much later, twenty-three years after the attack. Even those totally opposed to the death penalty would have found it difficult to object too strongly to the penalty in this instance, and as far as I recall, there was no world outcry to save them. In a way, it would have been heartless *not* to execute them, for it would have been an implicit minimisation of what they had done — though still I should not have wanted to act as their executioner myself. Can I ask anyone else to do on my behalf what I would not, because of moral qualms, do myself?

By very strange coincidence (but would it not be strange if, in a life which could be said to have consisted of scores of millions of events, there were no strange coincidences?), shortly after I had written the foregoing I happened upon a long article on the internet with the title *Japan's Secret Death Penalty Policy: Contours, Origins, Justifications, and Meanings*, by David T. Johnson, professor of sociology and law at the University of Hawaii.

---

[33] There was a peculiar syllogism in play:
I'd have to be mad to believe the doctrine to be true.
I'm not mad.
Therefore, the doctrine is true.

Professor Johnson is evidently a great expert on Japanese law and practice, which excites my admiration. He is a real scholar, who has devoted many years to his subject. (This article dates from 2006 and was published in the *Asia-Pacific Law and Policy Journal*.) For most people — except the Japanese, of course — mastery of Japanese would be achievement enough for a lifetime, let alone a mastery of Japanese law to boot. Perhaps Professor Johnson benefited greatly from having been brought up in Japan by American parents, such that mastery of Japanese was more natural to, than an accomplishment for, him.

Japan is one of the few liberal democracies that has retained the death penalty (some states of the USA and India being the others). It is strange also, is it not, that there is little outrage expressed in the western press about the retention by India and Japan of the penalty. It is almost as if no better could be expected of Indians and Japanese, lesser breeds without the law, as it was once put in the heyday of European imperialism. The death penalty is only to be expected of *them*, and therefore there is little point in protesting against it. We expect more of the Americans, however; but Professor Johnson does not share this condescension and judges the Japanese as he would judge anybody else. In this respect they, or at least their governors, do not come out well.

The death penalty is not carried out often in Japan — about four times a year — but it has public support which, not surprisingly, grew stronger after the trial of Shoko Asahara; and once it is admitted that the penalty is appropriate in one case, it is difficult to argue for its abolition on purely abstract ethical grounds. Most people would find it difficult to wax indignant about the execution of Asahara and his closest associates, albeit that they might think that the sentence should have been carried out sooner. (The only real objection came from a close relative of one of the victims, who said that the death penalty was too merciful for Asahara, and that he should have been made to suffer more and longer. It is mere prejudice that everyone would be better off if true justice were meted out.)

Professor Johnson focuses his paper of 64 pages on the secrecy that surrounds Japanese executions. The condemned man is held almost in isolation, and no one is allowed to visit him; he has no communication whatever with the outside world. He cannot talk even to his fellow prisoners who have been condemned to death. He is permitted spiritual consolation immediately before his execution but is not allowed to choose who his consoler will be. No relative or member of the public, no politician, is allowed to be present at his death (it seems odd to me that Professor Johnson should find this extraordinary). No one is informed of the day fixed for the execution: a bureaucratic decision, endorsed by the Minister of Justice, is suddenly carried out. The prisoner himself is not told. It could be any morning after the sentence is passed, but it is usually several years before it is carried out; the condemned man's lawyer is informed only *ex post facto*, as is his family, which is then given 24 hours to collect the body, which in most cases it refuses or is unable to do. Since only a minority of death sentences are carried out (even if most are not actually abrogated), the question arises as to the criteria by which the victims of the scaffold — execution in Japan is by hanging — are chosen, though in the case of Shoko

Asahara it is not difficult to guess.

The failure to inform the condemned man of the date of his execution seems cruel to the author, a wrong additional to that of the death penalty itself. The condemned man cannot say his goodbyes; he cannot make his peace with himself; every day, perhaps for many years, he experiences a terror at about eight in the morning, the time of execution. 'Will it be today?' he asks himself, hundreds and even thousands of times.

I am not sure that this is more cruel than telling a man that he is to be hanged tomorrow or in a week. We are all going to die: would we prefer to know the exact time, to the minute, when we shall do so? One of Asahara's senior lieutenants was assassinated, and at one point in the book above quoted, the authors say, 'He had only eighteen days to live.' We all have a fixed number of days to live, which will become clear to people only in retrospect, and never to us, though we are the people principally concerned. If I am to die in a road accident tomorrow, I have but one day to live, but I am not sure I would want to know this on the eve of the accident.

Professor Johnson says that support for the death penalty, in Japan as elsewhere, is maintained by the secrecy surrounding it. If the Japanese knew what hanging actually entailed, they would not favour it. Here again I am not sure that he is right. Public executions were, after all, popular public entertainments, and not only in distant historical times. Public executions of Nazi prisoners were conducted in the Soviet Union after the war, and in 1986, when I arrived in the city of Maiduguri in northeastern Nigeria, the streets were empty because everyone was away at the public executions. Nothing forced the people to attend, and indeed the television report that evening suggested that, the execution ground being waterlogged so that stakes could not be properly driven into it, there was the possibility of postponement, which would have disappointed the crowd. 'Fortunately', the report continued 'some dry land was found for the stakes.' Fortunate for some, perhaps, but not for all.

Professor Johnson says that ignorance of the procedure maintains support for executions, but perhaps ignorance of the details of the worst crimes also encourages abolitionists. If it is knowledge that the public needs to come to a 'correct' view of the death penalty, it needs knowledge of everything, including visual evidence of the crime. I point this out only because an argument must be balanced, for and against. I am against the death penalty because mistakes have been made in all jurisdictions, no matter how scrupulous; moreover, as I have intimated, I cannot ask others to do on my behalf what I would not do myself because of my moral objections to doing it.

The author also says that if executions are carried out in private, they could not exert the deterrent effect which is one of the justifications of the death penalty, but I am not sure that this is right either[34]. All that one needs to know for deterrence to work, if it does work, is the awareness that one *might* be executed, not that one for certain will be executed, or that one will be executed in public. I think the human imagination is strong enough for people not always to need concrete experience to guide or influence them.

---

[34] This was Doctor Johnson's argument in favour of public executions rather than executions *in camera*.

A man in his late thirties got on the train from Wolverhampton to London at Birmingham. He was dressed casually (who isn't, these days?), more or less like an aging adolescent. But he had intellectual hair, or perhaps I should say the hairstyle of an intellectual, and a highly intelligent face. He sat in a seat in the row in front of me, but on the other side of the gangway. He opened his computer as soon as he sat down. A name in large lettering appeared on the screen and I could not help reading it: *VOLKER PROTT*.

He then opened an academic-looking text, and out of curiosity I walked to the lavatory at the end of the carriage to see what it was about. The older I get, the idler my curiosity.

It was an article about the end of the GDR, the German Democratic Republic. I thought Mr Prott — probably Dr Prott — must himself be an academic and surmised that he might have written a book himself. I was right.

Perhaps those who come of age in the era of the smartphone will not think miraculous what I am about to recount, but for someone like me, brought up long before the internet was even dreamed of, it was nothing short of miraculous. I was able to establish, almost instantaneously, by means of my telephone that Dr Prott had written a book, *The Politics of Self-Determination: Remaking Territories and National Identities in Europe, 1917–1923*. Even more astonishingly, perhaps, I was able to order a copy in only an instant more. This will no doubt strike some people as an odd way of choosing reading matter, but at least the book was about a subject that interested me and in

147

fact remains extremely salient. I would not, however, have paid the full asking price for it — more than £100 ± but managed to find a copy, 'as new', for less than a quarter of that price. I thought I had better snap it up before anyone else did, though perhaps there were not very many other potential snappers-up of this book.

The Politics of Self-Determination was published by the Oxford University Press. It seemed to me that the Press followed the excellent business model of academic publishing in general. In the full knowledge that there were, say, a thousand libraries in the world that would feel obliged (and were able) to buy the title, the publisher was able to charge almost anything it likes, within some limit of reason, for the book, and therefore knew in advance what profit it would make on it. There was no risk whatever, and no need to go through a distributor and bookseller who would take a large percentage of the cover price. Not only money but effort would be saved, with certainty about the return on the money invested. No strenuous work need be expended on trying to sell the book to the general public, who would never buy it at such a price: any such effort would be pointless. And, of course, since the market was a captive one, there was no need either to take great care over the production standards of the product. In this respect, *The Politics of Self-Determination* was by no means the worst. It was nicely bound, the cover was good, and if the paper was not of the best quality and the margins were narrow, the typeface was at least agreeable to read. The most expensive copy I found was for sale at £232.

Is this business model exploitative? One's first inclination is to say that it is, and then to become pleasantly indignant. But exploitation is a concept that tends to recede as you approach it, like a mirage in the sand. Which of us in any commercial transaction does not seek his own best advantage? In times of food shortage, and when there is no hoarding, is it exploitative to raise prices to what the market will bear? It may be unfeeling and cruel, but that is not the same. And if not by price, how is scarcity to be allocated?

Dr Prott's book is somewhat on the dry side, but it is the dried fruit of wide, polyglot reading. German by origin, he did his doctorate in Italy, is clearly at home in French and wrote his book in English. It concerns the redrawing of the map of Europe after the end of the First World War, a problem to which no one could have found the perfect solution. President Wilson's idea of self-determination, seemingly cogent and coherent, came up against brute reality. Everything might have been simple if populations had been unmixed and all nationalities had been confined to exclusive territories, but such was far from the case. Even today, I do not mention in Hungary that the majority of the population of Transylvania is Romanian, nor when I am in Romania do I mention the strong Hungarian presence, contemporary and historical, in the province.

The book treats of two areas in particular: Alsace-Lorraine and Smyrna (Izmir) and its hinterland. As it happens, I have some connection with both through my wife. One of her aunts is Alsatian, who during the Occupation, when she was twelve or thirteen, was deported to Germany because her father was openly anti-German and anti-Nazi. Sent to Bavaria, she was not allowed to speak French and, as a new citizen of the Reich, was schooled in German. She was not ill-treated as an individual, but the deportation (she felt) affected her education adversely, and therefore her career path through life made more difficult. As a deportee, however, she did benefit from free transport in Paris for the rest of her life.

When in her late eighties she wrote a memoir longhand, her relatives had it printed for private circulation. It contained facsimiles of many documents, including a Nazi report that her father, a railwayman, was 'unreliable', having turned down better-paid work on political grounds.

Many of my wife's paternal relatives left Smyrna in 1922, though possibly before the mass population exchange between the Greeks and the Turks. My wife had supposed that she was therefore of half-Greek extraction (her father was born an Ottoman national), but DNA analysis carried out on one of her close relatives suggested an Armenian origin — though how far such analysis is to be believed I do not know. Among the family documents is a certificate of *Aryanité*, Arian-ness, for an uncle, provided by an Italian consul during the Occupation. One of her ancestors was a pioneer in France of silent movies, who for some reason failed to make the transition to the talkies. I am not much different from him: I am so attached to the book as a medium that I refuse to utilise the so-called social media, although it would be much to my advantage to do so, if to be widely known is an advantage.

Dr Prott established that no political dispensation based upon a simple principle of self-determination could have worked after the First World War (or indeed at any other time), and I suspect that he has a weakness for supranational solutions. The problem is that they probably cannot work either, at least not in the long run or without some element of coercion. In fact, man might be defined as a political animal without a political solution.

Attentive readers, if any such there be, will recall that I referred not long back to Joseph de Maistre's *Letters on the Spanish Inquisition*. I decided to read, or in one case to re-read, two long essays about him that I have in my library, written over sixty years ago at a short interval of one another. The first was by the French writer of Romanian origin, Emil Cioran, and the second by the British writer of Russian origin, Isaiah Berlin. Cioran's was written and published in 1978, and Berlin's written in 1960 but not published until 1990 because he thought it needed revision.

I used to admire Berlin's prose style greatly when I was younger, as I had Bernard Shaw's, but now when I read him again, I feel, as with Shaw when I re-read him, something of a revulsion. Berlin's style now seems to me to be that of an insufficiently controlled outpouring of a too fertile mind, as if his expression could not quite keep up with the pace of his thought. His adjectives and similes pour out torrentially; he is like a man in such a hurry that he will fall over himself. Berlin had the remarkable ability to extemporise a lecture for exactly the time at his disposal and make it sound as if it had been carefully prepared beforehand. This was an art of genius, and those who heard him always fell under his spell; but I am not sure that this remarkable facility served him well on the printed page. 'Too many spats, too many spats!' as someone (I forget who) once said on emerging from a meeting with

Mussolini early in the latter's career as head of government: or, perhaps more appositely, 'Too many notes!', as the Emperor Joseph is said to have said of Mozart's *Il Seraglio*. Too many words! Too many words! I cannot help thinking, when I read Isaiah Berlin.

Here, for example, is a sentence that seems to me to lose its way. Referring to Maistre's irrationalism, Berlin writes:

> ... the notion that if reason conflicts with common sense it must be treated like a prisoner, and expelled with curses on its head, is not compatible with any degree of respect for rational thought, the appeal is certainly not to experience, it is pure dogma used as a polemical battering ram...

The 'it' that is pure dogma refers presumably to the notion first mentioned, but by no means certainly. The sentence verges on eloquence divorced from meaning, and there are many other sentences with the same defect.

Given that Maistre was principally concerned to deny the gross simplifications of the Enlightenment; and that he emphasises man's inescapable irrationality, and hence the impossibility of his complete obedience to the dictates of reason; and that therefore the forces of unreason must be tamed somehow other than by pure argument if Man is to live in society, it is odd that Berlin should see in Maistre a forerunner of fascism but not of Freud, whose name appears nowhere in the essay. (After completing this sentence, I realised that it had a Berlinesque quality to it — and so I have left it, proving that Berlin may have had an influence on me after all.)

It gives me no pleasure to say so, but I think that Cioran's essay is the better of the two. It gives me no pleasure because I think that at the heart of Cioran's work in French is an unsaid but not entirely unconscious attempt to cover up, or at least to minimise, his past as a fellow-traveller of Romanian fascism — than which no fascism was more fascist. He presented himself as a man totally disabused, world-weary, deeply mistrustful of commitment to anything, I suspect because the one commitment of his life was to evil: and not just to evil, but to the most obvious and almost joyful evil. In his defence, it must be said that he was then a very young man. On the other hand, the evil was not very difficult to perceive.

Nevertheless, his essay on Maistre, subtitled *Essay on Reactionary Thought*, is interesting and even revealing, and written with talent. It begins:

> Among the thinkers, such as Nietzsche and St Paul, who had the taste and genius for provocation, there is a not negligeable place for Joseph de Maistre.

One might, of course, say the same for the author himself, who in the course of the essay says that the worst fate that can befall a writer is that he should be understood. If I were a purveyor of paradoxes, I should add that this is so of all humans whatsoever, not just of writers — at least, if all humans resemble me in any way, which I am inclined to believe.

When Cioran says that Maistre is an amalgam of theocrat and utilitarian, I think that he is right. The utilitarianism preceded the theocracy. Observing from afar, and reflecting on, what Lady Bracknell called the worst excesses of the French Revolution, he came to the not unreasonable conclusion that they stemmed ultimately from an intellectual source, namely the freedom to doubt, though whether the freedom followed the doubt or the doubt the freedom is a question for historians and perhaps also for metaphysicians. At question also is how far unity really existed in Christendom before the Reformation: the Hundred Years War, for example, preceded it. But here we are concerned not with truth itself, but with what Maistre took to be true.

At any rate, once freedom of thought became possible for many, it was inevitable, according to Maistre, that doubt and dissension would follow, while religious unanimity was essential to social peace. He thought that paganism and Mohammedanism (as he called Islam, not without reason, and as it was still known even in my childhood) were preferable to Protestantism because they promoted unanimity. The actual divisions within Islam did not bother him: the unanimity that was *claimed* by Islam was what counted for him.

I think fundamentalist Moslems might read Maistre with pleasure: not that they need to. They must have observed what happens to religion once the compulsion is removed. Under the microscope of reason, its doctrines come to many to seem absurd, not merely doubtful. They become the object of mockery once intellectual freedom is permitted, and if Islamic history is to be believed, Mohammed himself feared and detested mockery above all things. Like Maistre, the Islamic fundamentalist understands that, with religion, it is all or nothing, at least in the modern world. Tolerant religion is not really religion at all, but some kind of collective mummery masquerading as faith.

I have known one religiously observant person who observed the rites not because he believed in the truth of the doctrine on which they were founded but because without observance of some kind, almost of any kind, without intellectual questioning, mere anarchy is loosed upon the world.

Is this really so? The question is undecidable, for history has no finality, at least until the annihilation of mankind.

Few books have more telling titles than *The Demon of Progress in the Arts*, by Wyndham Lewis, who was one of the select few who successfully straddled two arts, that of painting and that of writing. He was original in both — original and disturbing. He developed his own style in painting which he called *Vorticism*, angular and geometric, poised between abstraction and figuration. It is striking rather than beautiful, the work of a man of talent, and gives one the impression that one has received a metaphorical splinter in the eye. He developed his style before the First World War, which suggests that western cultural disintegration was in progress before that war accelerated it.

The Demon of Progress was published in 1954, when Wyndham Lewis was 71. Not surprisingly, he had changed his mind about the need to be radical, or radically different, in art, a supposed need that led to what he thought was vacuity. I confess that his book does not seem to me to present a coherent argument, and it is difficult sometimes to know what exactly the author is trying to say. One gets almost as much from the title as from the whole book.

He calls the constant demand for novelty 'extremism': ideology at the time being more or less confined to Soviet communism. The balkanisation of ideology consequent upon the break-up of the Soviet Union had not yet occurred, and illegal actions in the name of protection of the environment, or other causes, had not yet attracted the admiration of young intellectuals. Wyndham Lewis analyses the causes of the rage for novelty in the visual arts and condemns it:

> … the extremism in the arts — most of all in the visual arts — is a pathological straining after something which boasts of a spectacular *aheadofness*, — looking upon the art in question as a *race*. In scientific techniques — in the manufacture of any machine, an automobile, an aeroplane, today more than ever it is a rival against the rival manufacturer, because things are so quickly outdated… but a race — a race to put as much distance as possible between himself [the artist] and what everyone else understands or enjoys, that is terribly silly.

As indeed it is. Artists (and many intellectuals in the humanities) suffer from science-envy because they feel that it is science and technology that are the most important determinants of modern life. Artists' studios are now sometimes called 'laboratories', as if the term would by itself give artists the kind of gravitas they desired, and that a mere studio could not give. But science — to make a most obvious point — has the controlling goal of truth to the natural world, an epistemological bottom line if you like, that art does not and cannot have. For there to be progress, there must be some objective goal, for example the cure of a previously incurable disease. Of course, there can be better and worse art, but later art cannot simply be assumed to be better than earlier, because it has supposedly progressed to a goal.[35]

Change is not progress unless there is a goal or end to which it moves. Unless the goal of painting is the mass sale of reproduced prints of paintings, Vladimir Tretchikoff, that great master of kitsch, cannot be said to have improved on Duccio. The defence of Tretchikoff, that he appealed to the taste of millions otherwise indifferent to art, seems to bear out, at least poetically, Wyndham Lewis's assertion in *The Demon of Progress* that 'the great majority [of the English population] are not culturally later than the Palaeolithic.' One hesitates or fears nowadays to write anything so implicitly anti-democratic — and incidentally, if it is true, it is true of nations other than the English. Disdain for the taste of others is dangerous if it is allowed to determine behaviour towards them, for people are divided by taste as much and as bitterly as by anything else, and to say of someone that his taste is bad is almost as hurtful

---

[35] It seemed to me that Mrs Thatcher made an analogous mistake when she wanted the inefficient public service in Britain to run on business lines in the hope of increasing efficiency according to business criteria. She wanted public servants to be business-like and turned them into businessmen, with all the perquisites, but none of the market discipline, of the latter. She did not realise that the incentives in the private and public sector had to be different. The predictable, though not predicted, result was the looting of the public purse by those employed in the public sector. She found the public service grossly inefficient and left it grossly inefficient and grossly corrupt.

as to say that he smells. I am reminded of something acute that Cioran said of Maistre: that reactionaries have licence to say what they truly think of man in the mass, whereas progressives have to pretend to approve of him and thereby do violence to their own secret thoughts, or to construct elaborate intellectual arguments to exculpate man in the mass from his unattractive qualities.

There is a danger both in this disdain for the common man and in the attempt to disguise it from oneself by denying it. The only solution is to keep it strictly under control while admitting its secret existence.

Wyndham Lewis's book might, with as much justification, have been titled *The Demon of Originality in the Arts*. Every person, by dint of being human, cannot help but be original, at least to an extent, though in many the responsibility conferred by inescapable uniqueness conflicts with the desire to escape it: hence the attraction for many of mass movements. But for those of artistic temperament, or at least ambition (who are more numerous), the desire to stand out is much greater, in theory, than the desire to melt into a crowd. Non-conformity is much easier than the creation of something genuinely worthwhile or valuable *sub specie aeternitatis*, and the conscious search for non-conformity leads only to conformity to a different standard. It is the cheapest form of originality, which should spring not from any desire to stand out, but from the need to express something which cannot be expressed in any other way. Originality should emerge from something other than the need or desire to be original.

Having spent some time recently on intellectually strenuous reading — strenuous by my standards, that is — and it being Christmas Eve as I write this, I gave myself permission to indulge in something lighter, and looking at my shelf of unread crime novels, of which there are quite a number, I alighted on *Murder of My Aunt* by Richard Hull, in one of those green Penguin paperback editions of my childhood (and before). I chose it because it started well and was written by a chartered accountant, whose profession one associates more with crime than with crime novels. Martin Edwards, the man who probably knows more about crime novels than any man who has ever lived, and whose massive tome on the subject I once reviewed, begins an article about Richard Hull, 'Although creative accounting is all too common, accountants who try their hand at creative fiction are a rare breed.'

There have been bankers, or those who worked in banks, insurance executives and mortgage managers among twentieth century poets (the century in which I still think that I live), but I can think of only one accountant other than Richard Hull (whose real name was Richard Henry Simpson), namely Sydney Fowler Wright, who was an author. Wright, who is now largely forgotten, was immensely prolific and wrote everything from political tracts and crime novels to literary biography and science fiction, He issued a prescient warning of the dangers of Nazism, *Prelude in Prague*, in the form of a novel.

Martin Edwards says that Hall, or Simpson, abandoned accountancy for full-time writing in 1934 after the success of *Murder of My Aunt*, his first book, while the potted biography on the back of the Penguin edition of 1953 says he continued in practice until 1939. Even the title of the book is not entirely stable: the more recent British Library edition is published as *The Murder of My Aunt*, not *Murder of My Aunt*. Here are two little mysteries that are not worth elucidating, except perhaps by someone with unpleasant thoughts, memories or emotions to keep at bay by means of mental occupation.

The plot of the book is simple but ingenious. Probably twists in the plot were more important in the 1930s than they are now, when psychological depth, or the appearance of it, is more appreciated. Certainly, sociological realism was not demanded in the 1930s, by which I mean sordidness. The taste then was for the crimes in crime novels to be committed in a milieu in which such crimes were not committed.

The majority of *Murder of My Aunt* is in the form of the protagonist's diary. Edward is a conceited, fat, greedy, lazy, stupid, pompous, self-important young man who is the ward of his detested Aunt Mildred, who has brought him up since the death of his parents in mysterious circumstances, the father having been a ne'er-do-well. The family are scions of minor gentry on the Welsh side of the border with England. Aunt Mildred makes Edward a small allowance, not large enough for him to live independently, and certainly not large enough for him to live in the style to which he would like to be accustomed, and to which he believes himself by birth entitled. To work would be demeaning for him, and in any case, no one would employ him because of his superior attitude to everything and everybody. His aunt keeps him on a tight rein, but he knows that in the event of her death he would inherit everything. An obvious motive for murder is supplied.

Edward despises Wales and would sell the ancestral home as soon as he inherited it: that the family has lived there for hundreds of years cuts no ice with him. (There is an interesting philosophical essay to be written, though not by me, on the political value or otherwise of multigenerational family pride, and its loss.) Edward sees no beauty in the surpassingly beautiful countryside of the Welsh Borders, for it offers him none of the urban pleasures and comforts that he so covets. The book opens with reflections on Welsh names, outlandish and unpronounceable to those who know no Welsh. The ancestral home is near the small (fictional) town of Llwll:

> How can any reasonable person live in a place that no Christian person can pronounce? One would like to begin at the beginning, but with Llwll you don't… One writer tells me that 'll' at the beginning of a word is pronounced like 'thl' with the 't' partially left out — a guide which is quite useless and unpracticable. Another one recommends a slight click at the back of the throat as if you were going to say 'cl' but were prevented apparently by someone seizing you by the throat. All I can say is that if whenever you are asked where you live, you seize yourself by the throat and start choking, it is apt to cause comment.

Certainly, Welsh names can cause difficulties to those who are not Welsh-speakers — who are only a third of the Welsh population. My wife and I recently drove through precisely the countryside of the fictional Llwll, and our satellite signal having been lost, we were obliged to navigate by maps. We were lost, and the problem was that the names of the villages through which we passed were so long and so alien that, no matter how slowly we drove, we could not make them out before we had passed them. Am I wrong in saying that anyone familiar with the Latin alphabet could spot at once the difference between, say, London and Brighton, but that the same cannot be said of Welsh village names? I should add that, far from annoying me, this idiosyncrasy delights me in a world growing ever more uniform.

Edward decides to do away with his aunt and his first effort, arranging for her to have an accident in her car by damaging the brake mechanism, very nearly succeeds. However, suspicion soon falls on him; and, unknown to him, his diary, in which he stupidly confides his plans for murder, has been read by his aunt. His next attempt is arson, which his aunt easily evades, and the third is to be by poison, aconite to be precise.

Edward's researches into poison interested me because, in the course of them, he writes of *Aconitum ferox* as well as of *Aconitum napellus*, the former being the Indian variety and the latter the European, which is the one usually used to poison people in Europe (*usual* is perhaps too strong a word for so rare an event).

Now it so happens that a friend of mine, Professor Ferner, was instrumental in a forensic triumph involving the distinction between the two. A certain man had all the symptoms of aconite poisoning before he died, but no aconite was found in his blood or body. Professor Ferner suggested that pseudo-aconite, the poison of Indian aconite, be looked for instead and bingo! There it was. Life — or death — had once again imitated art.

It is clear from Edward's diary that he will stop at nothing to kill his aunt. His aunt concludes that attack is the best form of defence and arranges a fatal accident for him by precisely the means by which he arranged a near-fatal car accident for her.

The last chapter is the aunt's account of all that has gone before. It is she who had edited Edward's diary, and it now remains for her to choose a title, a teasingly ambiguous one, for on first reading one would assume that she was the victim of the murder rather than its perpetrator. But, as she says, "of" can be a possessive, can't it? Can mean 'of or belonging to?'"

Clever. During the war, Hull, or Simpson, was employed to ensure that there was no fraud in government cost-accounting.

Having finished *Murder of My Aunt* on Christmas day, I thought I might take yet more time off from my current serious reading — the essays of the brilliant Victorian mathematician and philosopher, W.K. Clifford, on which I was engaged for a very different literary project. And it so happened that next to *Murder of My Aunt* on the shelf was another crime novel, in the same Penguin format, also unread by me, by the aforementioned chartered accountant, Sydney Fowler Wright, titled *Rex v. Anne Bickerton*. It was published in 1930 and republished by Penguin in 1947, under the title of *The King v. Anne Bickerton*.

S. Fowler Wright, as he was usually known, was born in

Smethwick, a town more famed for its race riots than as a cradle of literature. He left school for work at the age of 11. It is almost as surprising, therefore, that he became an accountant as that he became a translator of Dante and a biographer of Sir Walter Scott.

This was the first of Fowler Wright's crime novels, written when he was 46. It is certainly not one of the great crime novels, but, as it turned out, it had a special interest for me, on account of my obsessions and experiences. For one thing, the death is by arsenic poisoning, a favourite subject of mine, and for another, much of the action takes place in coroner's and assize courts. It is not quite a *roman à clef*, but I think I can identify the inspiration for at least three of the characters.

Once again, the plot is essentially simple even if the author, whose writing is workmanlike and sometimes ponderous rather than inspired, contrives to complicate it considerably.

A fractious, hypochondriacal, histrionic and capricious woman called Isabella Hackett[36] is poisoned to death in her bed by arsenic (of the cause of death there is no doubt, the government analyst, Sir Lionel Tipshaft, presumably modelled on the incontrovertible Sir William Willcox, the then famous toxicologist called in on all poison murders, having said so.) Mr Hackett is away on business in Liverpool at the time, and staying at the house at the time is his wife's sister, Miss Bickerton, whom Hackett dislikes. There is also Miss Dorling, who has been employed as a companion to the ever-ailing Mrs Hackett — but who is an old flame of Mr

---

[36] In character, she resembles Mrs Armstrong, wife of Herbert Rouse Armstong, who was hanged for having poisoned her to death with arsenic — or not, as the case may be.

Hackett with whom she is still in love.

Suspicion falls on Miss Bickerton, all the more strongly because Isabella Hackett, who often threatened suicide, has on a whim or in an access of anger, just written a will in her presence leaving her everything (which is quite a lot). She is arrested on suspicion of having put arsenious oxide in Isabella Hackett's tea, but it turns out to have been a prank by the nine-year-old boy next door. This is revealed at the last moment, not only to the readers but to characters themselves, just after the judge has finished his summing up in the case, clearly — but wrongly — indicating Miss Bickerton's guilt. If it had not been for a last-minute revelation, and with a very strong circumstantial case against her, he would have been found guilty and hanged. The book, then, is an implicit argument against the death penalty, a plea for its abolition, which is all the more surprising, perhaps, because Fowler Wright was an ardent conservative, even reactionary.

That the book is such a plea is suggested by the veiled reference to the cases of Greenwood and Armstrong, two Welsh solicitors accused of arsenic murders, the first having been acquitted and the second condemned, in part, so it has been suggested, by an official determination that two accused persons in succession should not escape the gallows. The author hints that this is a motive for the prosecution of Anne Bickerton, for she has been previously acquitted of a similar crime.

There is yet further evidence. The judge in Armstrong's case was Lord Justice Darling, and the judge in this book is clearly a portrait of him. He is called Mr Justice Ackling, a bachelor like Darling, and is so unmistakably him that only a defence of truth could have saved the author in an action for libel. The portrait is an extremely unfavourable one and implies that the judge is very set on hanging people — as, indeed, Darling was alleged to have been. When Miss Bickerton's acquittal becomes inevitable, on the mere grounds that she is innocent:

> Mr Justice Ackling would have been a much happier man (though he would not have admitted it, even to himself) had he been pulling out the black cap which he had put in his pocket that morning...[37]

Fowler describes Ackling exactly as Darling was, or was reputed to have been:

> Mr Justice Ackling had a wide knowledge of law, and a passion for the conviction and punishment of the unfortunates who were brought before him.
>
> It would not be exactly an injustice, but it would be an inaccuracy of diagnosis, to suggest that he was indifferent to the guilt or innocence of those whom he tried and sentenced... But as a rule he went on the assumption that the dock was the place for criminals, and he relied upon the police to see that a selected criminal filled it as surely as that his man-servant (he was an unmarried man)

---

[37] The black silk square which judges placed on the crowns of their wigs as they passed sentence of death. When a friend of mine was appointed a High Court judge, he was given one though the penalty had long been abolished. Perhaps someone expected, or hoped, that it might return.

would put tea, and not cacao or coffee, in his morning teapot... The criminal will naturally wriggle. If he is a murderer he may wriggle very hard indeed. He may have paid experts to assist his efforts, But it will be the duty, and perhaps the pleasure, of Mr Justice Ackling to see that he doesn't wriggle free.

As for the accused, Miss Bickerton, she is a colourless creature and in describing her, Fowler lets rip, or fly, with his opinion of much of humanity. She was one of those 'who will never meet a wind that is too strong, or be drowned by any turn of tide, for they will never leave the shore.' They 'play for safety from birth; they hide deep in the crowd; they tremble lest the chance of a moment's forgetfulness should bring some passing publicity, some trivial penalty upon them. They would be agonized to walk abroad in an unusual colour or a coat of a new cut. Far from resenting the pressure of the social order that brands and limits and constrains, they would willingly be held in yet closer bondage, if they could thereby gain a more complete obscurity, a greater restriction of opportunities either to risk or decide.'

Not bad, I think, for a man who left school aged 11, and still true, though the conformist fear of appearing conformist has replaced Miss Bickerton's kind. And a few other points I would like briefly to make before leaving *The King v. Anne Bickerton* to its mouldering oblivion. Fowler is very good on the subject of whether such as Mrs Hackett, a histrionic hypochondriac, really believe what they are saying, or even whether they know whether they believe it. Second, the arsenic that killed Mrs Hackett was in the form of powdered weedkiller, as it was in the Armstrong case. And third, Winson Green Asylum (later renamed All Saints' Hospital, now closed) and Winson Green Prison figure prominently in the book. I worked as a doctor for fifteen years in Winson Green Prison.

There may be more powerful novellas than Lydia Chukovskaya's *Sofia Petrovna*, but surely not many.

Its history as a literary artifact is very remarkable and its survival almost miraculous. Just before the Siege of Leningrad[38], the author entrusted her manuscript, a single handwritten copy in a school exercise book, to a friend when she herself was evacuated to Tashkent. Like scores of thousands of others, this friend died of starvation during the siege, but on the day prior to his death, he in turn entrusted the manuscript to someone who survived, as did the manuscript. The gesture of the dying man was a magnificent act of faith not only in the future, but of the vital importance of literature in that future.

Naturally, it was extremely dangerous to keep the manuscript while Stalin was still alive, but all bad things, as with good, must come to an end, and Stalin died. Still, it was only ten years later, after the relative thaw under Khruschev, that publication of *Sofia Petrovna* could even be contemplated. In fact, it was accepted for publication, typeset and ready for sale and distribution, when there was an ideological freeze

---

[38] About which I have recently written in these pages.

again, and it was withdrawn from publication. Finally, it was published in 1966 first in French and then in English in 1967. It was not, however, published where it most was needed, Russia, until 1988.

Sofia Petrovna is the widow of a doctor who has one son, Kolya (Nikolai). Of bourgeois social antecedents, they now live in one room of the flat that the family once owned, the other rooms each occupied by a family. (A friend of mine was brought up in just one such flat in Moscow in the 1950s and 60s.)

At the opening of the novella, life in Leningrad before the assassination of Kirov[39] seems almost normal, or at least bearable. There are little pleasures available such as pastries and ice-cream, even if accommodation is cramped and overcrowded. Sofia Petrovna works as the head of a typing pool at a publishing company — if company is quite the word. Her son, Kolya, who is the apple of her eye, is a student of engineering, fully indoctrinated in the Soviet ideology, to the extent of believing that the expropriation of the family property, in which they have been allocated a single room, was justified by the demands of social justice. He is confident that the Soviets are building a new and better world.

He and his close friend, Alix (Finkelstein), also an engineer, are sent to a factory in Sverdlovsk, formerly (and now once again) Yekaterinburg, where the Tsar and his family were murdered in 1918. There, Kolya invents a new machine and is praised on the front page of *Pravda*, to the delight and pride

---

[39] Sergei Kirov, head of the Communist Party in Leningrad, was assassinated in 1934, probably on Stalin's orders. The assassination was made a pretext for a wave of even greater repression than ever.

of his mother. Kolya writes home regularly to his mother, but his letters are strangely impersonal.

The atmosphere at the publisher's changes after Kolya's arrest as a 'wrecker' and 'terrorist'. As the mother of an accused person, Sofia Petrovna is herself suspect whom it becomes toxic to know. In any case, denunciation and suspicion have become universal, affecting everyone. Today's model citizen becomes tomorrow's enemy of the people, and the fact that Kolya had not been denounced long before his arrest becomes grounds for an ever-widening circle of suspicion. Arrests follow, and the arrested disappear into the maw of the penitentiary system. Relatives of the disappeared spend days and nights queuing in atrocious conditions at the offices of the various authorities, trying to discover the whereabouts and charges against their relatives, and trying also to pass on the money or clothes that they will need.

Sofia Petrovna, herself a firm believer in the justice and benevolence of the Soviet system in general and of Stalin in particular, thinks at first that there must have been some mistake — all systems make mistakes — in Kolya's arrest. After all, she knows him to be innocent. Eventually, however, she manages to reach the prosecutor, who informs her that Kolya has confessed his crimes and been sentenced to ten years' exile without right of correspondence.[40] The prosecutor tells her that it is no part of his job or responsibility to tell her where he has been exiled to. Sofia then has an irresolvable conflict in her mind between her belief in Kolya's innocence

---

[40] Though she did not know this, such a sentence was, in fact, a penalty of death.

and the fundamental justice of the Soviet system. She cannot believe in his guilt but cannot believe either in the inhumanity, the arbitrariness, the injustice of the system that sentenced him. All the others who have been arrested, she thinks, must be guilty, though it is perfectly obvious that they are as innocent as Kolya.

On rumours of the release of a few prisoners, she persuades herself that Kolya has also been released, has returned to his factory to work and will soon be sent to Crimea for a holiday, after which he will return to Leningrad to be reunited with her, having in the meantime married. Sofia Petrovna has neglected herself for over a year, depressed by Kolya's arrest and sentence, and now she tidies up the room and herself in anticipation of his return. She has been sacked from her job because of the notion of collective responsibility (which was still operative in Albania when I visited that country), her guilt being that her son was a traitor and her father a former landowner and colonel in the Tsarist army. She has absolutely no evidence that Kolya has been released but goes about her preparations for his return in a state of deluded euphoria. She tells people that her son has been released, and they congratulate her, not realising that she is mad. Previously, they had been too frightened to pass the time of day with her, but now that they think that Kolya has been released, it is safe to talk to her again.

Sofia Petrovna is recalled to reality when, for the first time in more than a year, she receives a letter from Kolya. It has clearly been smuggled because it contains assertions, such that his confession was false and was beaten out of him, that no censor would have allowed through. She considers using the letter as a basis of complaint but realises that this would achieve nothing but her own deportation. She burns the precious letter.

She describes with brilliant concision the development of the atmosphere of fear, terror, distrust and denunciation. It didn't take long, especially where *Homo sovieticus* had already become the predominant type. This type had taken only twenty years to emerge after the Revolution. I should add that when Lydia Chukovskaya wrote this novella, her own husband, the physicist Matvei Bronstein, had been arrested and, unknown to her, shot — she thought he had been exiled for ten years, as Sofia Petrovna thought that her Kolya had been.

Well, you might say, all this happened in the Soviet Union in the 1930s. What relevance has it for us now? People ask the same question about, say, the Rwandan genocide. After all, that was in Africa...

True enough, we have experienced nothing comparable. Still, there are small clouds on the horizon. Occasionally, people are dismissed from their work for expressing an opinion contrary to the current orthodoxy, and worse still, must express enthusiasm for that orthodoxy to obtain the job in the first place. An atmosphere of fear exists in many organizations, albeit not of the fatal consequences of denunciation, as in the Soviet Union. But one ought never to forget that denunciation is a pleasure and to do harm to others in the name of a greater good, however illusory, a great delight to a certain type of person, a type never in short supply. We are never more than a decade away from that which Lydia Chukovskaya so brilliantly depicts.

If she had written nothing else, *Sofia Petrovna* would have justified her whole life.

Although Chukovskaya says in the introduction to her book that no other contemporaneous novel of the repression in Russia of the 1930s exists, her friend, Anna Akhmatova, considered one of the greatest Russian poets of the twentieth century, wrote a long poem, or series of poems, about it, called *Requiem.*

Alas, I can read it only in translation, and poetry is what is lost in translation. Translators are faced by the impossible choice between literal fidelity and fidelity to poetic truth, which is an amalgam of rhythm, diction, metaphor, atmosphere, and the indefinable. There are no 'correct' translations of poetry, only translations with different shortcomings. Of course, some shortcomings may be worse or more obtrusive than others, but every translation must be open to objection. But if no translation were ever to be attempted because none will be perfect and all will be unsuccessful, the poets of every language must forever remain in not-so-splendid, linguistic isolation.

The translator of my edition of *Requiem* was D.M. Thomas, the novelist. He was taught Russian in the army during his National Service in the 1950s, when the armed forces needed Russian-speakers to read the Soviet press, listen to broadcasts and intercept radio messages (one of the disadvantages of speaking the world's *lingua franca* being that so many foreigners understand it). The armed forces, like the communist countries themselves, taught languages extremely well, much better than do our universities. I knew a man who, without any academic distinction, was taught Russian very well in the RAF, and still read and spoke it fluently. The armed forces applied aptitude tests before deciding whom to train, and security checks as well. (As a student aged about 20, MI6 came to interview me about a friend of mine, a brilliant student of Russian, whom I suppose they were hoping to recruit. I was very naïve at the time and must have struck MI6 as an innocent — all to the good as far as my testimony was concerned.)

It is no criticism of the translator or of Akhmatova herself that I was less moved by *Requiem* than by *Sofia Petrovna*, though the authors had similar stories. Akhmatova's husband, the poet Nikolai Gumilev, was executed by the Bolsheviks in 1921. By then she had been separated from him for three years. Her son, Lev, was arrested in 1935, and spent nearly two decades in the Gulag. Her common-law husband, Nikola Panin, was also arrested, released, and rearrested after the war, dying in the Gulag. Here was material for complete silence, for despair or for suicide — or for narration, or in Akhmatova's case, for poetry. The problem for other writers that she poses is that she makes all their material, all their experience, seem shallow and almost frivolous by comparison.

This is no doubt absurd: literature does not live by catastrophe alone, nor is joy any the less real because of the existence of despair. Yet perhaps because my own mother experienced a catastrophe not dissimilar in type from Chukovskaya's and Akhmatova's, never speaking about it rather than writing about it, and because after her death I discovered something so terrible, so discreditable to the human race, in the papers of whose existence I had previously been unaware, and about which I shall never write, I sometimes feel that catastrophe is the only true subject for a writer. This is like rejecting the art of cookery because there are hungry people in the world.

Akhmatova's *Requiem* covers much the same ground as *Sofia Petrovna* — or is it the other way round? In the prefatory note she wrote in 1957, when the worst of the terror was over, but Russia was still far from free, Akhmatova said, 'In the fearful years of the Yezhov terror, I spent seventeen months in prison queues in Leningrad', just like Chukovskaya's Sofia Petrovna. One day, someone in the queue guessed that she was a writer or poet of some sort:

> Beside me, in the queue, was a woman with blue lips. She had, of course, never heard of me; but she suddenly came out of that trance so common to us all and whispered in my ear (everyone spoke in whispers there): 'Can you describe this?' And I said, 'Yes, I can.' And then something like the shadow of a smile crossed what had once been her face.

The fact that one day it would be written about was consolatory to the woman: here one thinks of Primo Levi's fear that one day no one would be interested in, or believe, what he set out to describe. But that the abomination would not be forgotten, that it would be immortalised in words, was reassuring (if only to a minor extent): that all the suffering would not go unremarked and that the narration would serve as some kind of posthumous punishment of those responsible for it, this was almost a consolation. The words restore meaning to the world and would be a refutation of the camp guard's fathomlessly nihilistic statement that 'Here there is no *Why*.'

'What was once her face': no five words could more concisely capture what depth of suffering, over a prolonged period, can do to someone, suffering that is not the consequence of what used to be called 'natural evil' — earthquake, say, or volcano — but of the malignity of one's fellow creatures.

From the purely literary point of view, the cataclysms wrought by Lenin, Stalin, Hitler, Mao, Pol Pot, had one advantage: they rendered exaggeration impossible. Accounts might be well or less well written, but there could be no straining after emotional impact as there is, say, on Coleridge. What were his romantic agonies to set beside what Akhmatova wrote:

> In those years, only the dead smiled,
> Glad to be at rest!

Leningrad was then 'a needless appendage of its prisons' — as if oppression, denunciation, incarceration, torture, were its principal or only business, its very *raison d'être*.

Just as Sofia Petrovna's fictional son was arrested, so was Anna Akhmatova's. Just as had Sofia Petrovna, so Anna Akhmatova, a woman of great refinement, spent years trying to obtain news of him:

For seventeen months I've called you
To come home, I've pleaded
– O my son, my terror! – grovelled
At the hangman's feet.

Lev Gumilev (her son) was in fact released to fight in the Soviet army. But in 1949 he was rearrested and not released for another seven years. Once released for good, he became an ethnographer and political geographer. His idea — Eurasianism — was later to be much favoured by a well-known Russian political figure, Vladimir Putin. Akhmatova wrote:

Stars of death stood
Above us, and innocent Russia
Under bloodstained boots...

Innocent Russia, indeed! And not only innocent Russia, alas.

I am not so much a collector as an accumulator of books. Nevertheless, there are among my books some subjects more highly represented than could be accounted for by chance. They could not really be called a collection but all the same are quite numerous. A real collector would have more; someone with a special interest in the subject would have fewer.

Among the abovementioned subjects is Russia from 1917 to the 1950s, with an especial concentration on the 1920s and

30s. There are many eye-witness accounts of Russia by literary figures who spent a few weeks there: Theodore Dreiser, H.G. Wells, Liam O'Flaherty, for example. They returned from their trips to write books about what they had seen or thought that they had seen. There are books of praise — *Soviet Russia Fights Crime, Russia Fights Neurosis* — and books of condemnation — *The Red Terror, Red Dusk and the Morrow*. It is interesting to read their prognostications, which are a warning to the wise against the temptations of prognostication.

Many years ago, I bought a small book by Bertrand Russell, *The Practice and Theory of Bolshevism*, published in 1920. My copy once belonged to E. StC. Pemberton, who inscribed his name in it with an italic pen in a hand not lacking in confidence. From a brief search on the internet, without the assistance of which I should never have found the following, I discovered that the owner had been Colonel Ernest St Clair Pemberton (1857–1950). In a book about the owners of country houses, the historian, antiquarian, novelist, diarist and aesthete, James Lees-Milne describes a horrible visit to Pemberton, whom he describes as 'as a fiendish old imbecile who has an inordinate opinion of himself and his own judgment.'

Perhaps this judgment was itself a little hasty, for in an obituary of him in the *Somerset County Herald and Taunton Courier* of the 30 December 1950, we learn that he was first in his class of engineers in the army in 1877, and was 'a good linguist' who became Russian interpreter for the army, and 'who made some remarkable journeys in Russia and Siberia… The last of his twelve visits to Russia was made when he was about 80.' He was chosen to represent the army at the funeral of Tsar Alexander III: not altogether an imbecile, then.

Interestingly, though, the obituary made no mention of his character, other than that he was 'a singularly erect figure even in great old age', and there are no expressions of regret, even perfunctory, at his passing. But I think we may conclude that, given his long interest in Russia, his reading of Russell's book was probably more than casual. He would have been an interesting man to talk to.

Russell's book seems to me confused. Clearly, it was scribbled very quickly, for it was published in the year of the author's visit to Russia, which took place from May 11 to June 16, and the preface was completed in September. One chapter, by far the worst written, was actually by his secretary, destined to be his second wife, D.W. (Dora) Black, an upper-middle class feminist and socialist, who believed in open marriages but nevertheless divorced Russell later for his infidelity.

Some of Russell's opinions seem to me simplistic to the point of puerility. They were not developed as a result of what he saw on his journey but were those he held before he set on it. He tells us that he is a Communist, but not in the Marxist sense; rather that there should be an equal distribution of wealth, even though he also says that economic inequality in itself does not seem to him very important. In that case, then, one might have thought the establishment of such communism couldn't have been very important, either. He doesn't pause to consider whether property held in private might not be a precondition of political freedom.

He is clear enough about the defects of Bolshevism, however. He had an hour's conversation with Lenin, whom he did not like very much: 'He struck me as too opinionated and narrowly orthodox.' Moreover, 'Love of liberty is incompatible with whole-hearted belief in a panacea for all human ills.' Russell continued, 'Trotsky made more of an impression on me from the point of view of intelligence and personality, but not of character... his vanity was even greater than his love of power.'

Russell described the totalitarianism that already existed in Russia after only two and a half years. The problem, he thought, was inherent in Bolshevism and not the product of circumstances:

> The Bolshevik theory is that a small minority are to seize power and are to hold it until Communism is accepted practically universally, which they admit may take a long time. But power is sweet, and few men surrender it voluntarily... and the habit becomes most ingrained in those who have governed by bayonets, without popular support. Is it not almost inevitable that men placed as the Bolsheviks are in Russia... will be loath to relinquish their monopoly of power, and will find reasons for remaining until some new revolution ousts them? Will it not be fatally easy for them... to decree large salaries for high government officials...? The system created by violence and the forcible rule of a minority must necessarily allow of tyranny and exploitation... The Government has a class-consciousness and a class-interest quite distinct from those of the genuine proletarian, who is not to be confounded with the Government... I see no reason whatever to expect equality or freedom to result from such a system.

Russell's attachment to Communism remains, however. He thinks it can come about peacefully and suggests that self-management of industry would be a beginning: for if industries were managed by workers in their own interests, not only would the result be fairer and more just, but more efficient, inasmuch as every worker in an industry would have an incentive to work hard and efficiently, which he thought was far from the case when he wrote.

With regard to the Bolsheviks, Russell wrote 'There must be administration, there must be officials who control distribution…' But this must be the case also under any form of communism whatever, except the primitive, pre-industrial type. Moreover, in any large enterprise, administrative power cannot be equalised. People vary not only in capacity but in ambition. Not every decision can be taken on a vote of everyone. But for Russell, industrial self-management is in any case only the first stage in the peaceful 'progress' towards full Communism.

There are many contradictions in Russell's book, no doubt in part the consequence of his rush to publication. He tells us that the Marxian theory, that economic class interest is the explanation of all that happens in history, is wrong, and that religion and nationalism are just as strong factors, but he accepts that capitalism was responsible for the recent World War (of which Russell was a brave opponent). He also says that, 'The war and its sequel have proved the destructiveness of capitalism' and 'that Communism might have its power to heal the wound that the old evil system has inflicted on the human spirit,' albeit that Bolshevism is 'destined to bring upon the world centuries of darkness and futile violence.'

This all seems very muddled to me, especially in a logician, though it must be remembered that logic has never guided history, which is made by what he calls 'fiendish old imbeciles'[41] — or even worse, by fiendish young imbeciles.

I think I may say without undue boasting that I was one of the first publicly to remark on the ascent of tattoos up the social scale.

I first became interested in the phenomenon of tattooing when I worked as a doctor in a prison. I quickly noticed that at least nine-tenths of white prisoners were tattooed. In those days, their tattoos were amateurish, all in India ink. Many had been done in prison itself and were of simple design, often with words such as *Made in England* round a nipple or *Cut here* above a dotted line round a neck. I recall a small man with the words *No Fear* in thick black capitals on the side of his neck above the collar line, which was occasionally taken as a challenge by someone in the pub, and on one occasion led to him being dealt a fractured skull. Another prisoner had a tattoo on the inside of his forearm of a policeman hanging from a lamppost, which I doubt served him well when he was taken down the station.

My one contact with the phenomenon of tattooing before working in the prison was at Speaker's Corner in Hyde Park in the early 1960s. There, among the socialists, the vegetarians

---

[41] Precisely the locution used of the former owner of the book, Colonel Pemberton.

and the friar from the Catholic Truth Society, was a man who did not speak but rather simply took his shirt off to reveal a body whose every inch was covered in tattoos, red and blue. I remember still his enigmatic smile, and he amazed the little crowd gathered around him, who obviously regarded him as a freak rather than as a harbinger of things to come. Nowadays, he would hardly be worth a glance: he was the David Beckham of his time.

In the 1990s, however, more professional tattooing spread rapidly, and with it the elaboration of the designs employed. There was no doubt that tattooing became highly skilled, but skill is not self-justifying. Safe-breaking is a skill, but one would not wish it to spread. Forgery and fraud of all kinds are skills and killing to order can be a skill. Though tattoos became ever more complex and elaborate, they retained one uniting characteristic: they were all kitsch. Their aesthetic sensibility was precisely that of the majority of prisoners who start to draw once they are imprisoned.

When I first saw educated, middle-class persons having themselves tattooed, I assumed, or hypothesised, that they were expressing sympathetic identification with the poor and marginalised, and therefore, in their own eyes at least, their act or gesture was one of generosity of spirit or political virtue. This irritated me — real virtue is not so cheaply bought — but I realised soon enough that if ever my hypothesis had been correct, it soon ceased to be, for before long one-third of the adult population was tattooed.

I did, however, notice in all the increasing number of books on the subject (I started a small collection of them) that the advance of tattooing both numerically and in sophistication was regarded as a triumph of freedom of personal expression: self-expression being the highest form of expression possible.

Therefore, when I read a review of a collection of poems titled *The Tattoo Collector*, by a young Hong Kong Chinese woman, resident in Scotland, called Tim Tim Chang, I thought that I should buy it, not because I had high hopes for the quality of its poetry, but because of my interest in the fashion for tattooing. A photograph on the cover showed a young woman with her left shoulder and chest, as far as revealed, completely covered by a tattoo.

A recent survey of tattooing in the United States found that tattooing was (surprisingly) most common among blacks than among whites, and more common among whites than among Asiatics — a strange category given the great variation among the latter. In other words, there was an inverse relationship with educational and economic success. Correlation, of course, is not causation.

Tim Tim Chang moved from Hong Kong to Edinburgh, largely to escape the oppressive atmosphere of her native city. For her, perhaps, a tattoo represented freedom, but for me it represented bad taste and as much a desire to conform as to resist conformity.

Much of her poetry is, to me, undecipherable. It employs techniques which were extra-poetical, such as startling arrangements of words on the page, or print with faint ink with occasional words or parts of words printed in bold. I am, of course, a kind of brontosaurus where literary taste is concerned, but this seems to me pretentious, a straining after significance that the words alone could not convey.

Most of her poems, though, are arranged somewhat more

normally, and can even remind one of Sylvia Plath:

> I would love to believe the sky
> is apologising but it never does.
> We rain on its behalf...

Or 'We mourn every day, We are good at it now.'

Mainly I was interested in the poems about tattooing, however, for their psychological rather than their literary interest. What does a tattooed person think that he or she is doing, or expressing, by means of his self-mutilation (as I think it)? What is it that drives 42 per cent of French adults aged between 25 to 40 to undergo what is still a painful process?

The poet looks at jars — what medical students used to call pots — in the anatomical museum of Edinburgh Medical School, containing body parts. In a prose poem titled, significantly, *Skin Me*, she writes:

> Here a black star that stops smudging was someone's shoulder, now a waxy bookmark... Here, the more marked you are the easier it is to identify you...

The word 'you' is printed on the right-hand side of a line separated from the rest of the text — typographical narcissism.

Here, perhaps, is a clue to the motive, or one of the motives, of the tattooed: a desire for individuation in a mass society in which the inescapable uniqueness of every human being is not felt strongly enough. You must proclaim your difference, even if by doing so you proclaim yourself at the same time the member of a tribe, class or group.

In the opening poem of the collection, *The Tattoo Collector*, one of three poems of that title, the poet says:

> I'm convinced if I turn my blank slate
> into a puzzle, an exhibit, you'll be looking
> and not looking at me…

The tattoo is the visual equivalent of psychobabble, that form of speech in which a person talks endlessly of himself while revealing nothing specific. In the same poem occur the lines:

> Needs to needle. Blessed are the pains
> that numb other pains.

But what are the pains that can be numbed by having oneself tattooed? Surely, they must be superficial — or one has a superficial idea of one's own psychology? In the third of the poems with the same title, the poet remarks, 'Strange how tattoos stay on mummies.' The last stanza goes:

> the tattooist must observe
> your erratic dapples for hours
> to design something lasting
> to capture your skin's weather.

Here is a desperate search for meaning or significance. One imagines oneself a mummy, found five thousand years hence. One's tattoos immortalise. This is the tragedy of superficiality in search of depth.

Most people, I imagine, have been irritated at some time by a telephone call from an unknown person, representing an unknown company, trying to sell an unwanted product: a new heating system, say, or new window frames.

I try to be polite to such a person, reminding myself that behind the nuisance there is a human being, probably one who detests his work but must make a living somehow and who is paid a pittance unless he succeeds in selling something to someone: in short, a person of desperation.

Publisher's publicists are no doubt one rung up the ladder from telephone salesmen. Their job is to interest reviewers in a new book when thousands of others are published monthly. I don't know what evidence there is that they are worth their pay (to the publisher), but sometimes in my case they succeed — in my capacity as book reviewer, I hasten to add, not that of author of books. I think they work on the supposition that there is no such thing as a bad review, complete silence — falling dead-born from the press, in Hume's memorable phrase about his own great work — being far worse.

One publicist in particular contacts me with some regularity, though I am not so influential a person that many bother to do so. More than once, it has worked — for her. Recently, she contacted me about a book by Gérald Garutti, translated from the French, titled *Il faut voir comme en se parle: Manifeste pour les arts de parole*, published in English as *Watch Your Words: A Manifesto for the parts of Speech*.

The author is clearly a gifted man. He is a theatre director both in Paris and London, has translated *Richard III* into

French, has a doctorate in literature and has taught at Cambridge. He is clearly also a man of goodwill, and it therefore pains me to say when, having been in France at the time the publicist drew my attention to his book, I bought it in the original, I found it full of clichés. Its good intentions were saccharine and its form rather like an extended speech to the party faithful by Messrs Blair or Sarkozy. Many short sentences without verbs. An accumulation of connotations without denotations. Well-meaning assertions impermeable to criticism. A flood of words tedious to analyse in detail. Perhaps this is how people think nowadays.

The author starts from the observation, surely correct (or at least I agree with it), that the quality of public expression in words has deteriorated of late — though at what precise date *of late* became *of late* is, no doubt, partly a function of the length of one's life and memory. We live, he says, in a world of sound and fury. In typical fashion — typical for him, that is — he goes on to say 'A world of rumours, tweets, hashtags and clashes… Of battles, of lols and of likes… A world of networks, in which we kill for a word.' Rarely for verbs.

I have long thought that nothing is worth saying, at any rate in expository prose, unless it is worth contradicting. (I leave aside the question of whether I include this assertion.) Towards the end of the book, we read:

> We need to listen. We need to be present. We need a story in common. We need dialogue. We need meaning. We need understanding. We need nuance. We need authenticity, We need beauty. We need truth. We need benevolence. We need love. We need humour. We need

dignity. We need encounters. We need exchanges. We need respect. We need attention. We need consideration. We need interactions. We need mastery. We need precision. We need justice. We need expression. We need elaboration.

Et cetera, et cetera. Though we must be precise, we need not specify what we must be precise about. Would anyone say that, in general, we do not need to listen? On the other hand, we do not need to listen at all times and all places. Indeed, there are times when we need not to listen. And who can be found to deny the need for love? Who would deny that a sense of humour is desirable, though it can sometimes be misplaced?

There are the usual, or at any rate frequent, evasions in the book, a failure to recognise that in all history there have been irreconcilable differences between people and groups of people, and that, however long we may live at peace and find common ground, this is unlikely ever to be perpetual. Dialogue is like corruption according to the late marshal Mobutu Sese Seko: it requires two to engage upon it, and one of the pair may refuse. Knowing at what point our differences are irreconcilable, when we can no longer tolerate the intolerant, requires judgment, which is always fallible and sometimes catastrophically so. Such is the price of being human.

It so happens that, while reading this book, I tidied a pile in my library, among them the second volume of Bishop Butler's works, published in 1897 and edited by William Ewart Gladstone, then in retirement from his Premiership (I hope that we do not have to look forward to Keir Starmer's literary efforts when he leaves office, and rather doubt it). Flicking through this volume, that of Bishop Butler's printed sermons, I noticed the fourth of them titled *Upon the Government of the Tongue*.

What a pleasure it was to read the Bishop's measured prose after the breathlessness of M. Garutti! Here, for example, is the beginning of the author's preface to his collected sermons, published in 1729:

> Though it is scarce possible to avoid judging in some way or other of almost everything that's itself to one's thoughts; yet it is certain that many persons, from different causes, never exercise their judgment, upon what comes before them, in the way of whether it be conclusive and holds. They are perhaps entertained with some things, not so with others; they like, and they dislike; but whether that which is proposed to be made out be really made out or not; whether a matter be stated according to the real truth of the case, seems to the generality of people merely a circumstance of no consideration at all.

In his sermon on the government of the tongue, Butler warns us against the propensity to talk for the sake of talking. This is not so minor a vice as might be supposed (says Butler), because, among other things, 'when subjects [of a neutral kind] are exhausted, they [the overtalkative] will goeth to defamation, scandal, divulging of secrets, their own secrets as well as those of others, anything rather than be silent. They are plainly hurried on by the heat of their talk to say quite different things from what they first intended and which they afterwards wish unsaid; or improper things which they had no other end in saying, but only to afford employment to their tongues.'

Butler is against self-expression as a good in itself. With admirable succinctness, he gives rules for 'government of the tongue', a little reminiscent of Orwell's for the writing of good prose. They are a) to esteem silence; b) to eschew talebearing and c) not to court attention.

Is it not strange that an English clergyman of three centuries ago should speak to us more pointedly, in our age of democratic, not to say demotic, logorrhoea, than an esteemed intellectual of our own time?

Recently, two people close to me have suffered great pain, one as a result of natural evil (as it was called in the eighteenth century) and the other as a result of unfathomable human malignity. There are, of course, perfectly ordinary explanations for both, but neither of the sufferers could be said to have deserved their pain.

The first, who was struck by illness, had always lived healthily and had avoided those things or that conduct that might have caused or at least brought forward his illness, the second a victim of crime that seemed almost random, the result of motiveless malignity, as Coleridge mistakenly said of Iago. The first had 'bad' heredity with respect to his illness, and the second was, as the British police now put it, 'in the wrong place at the wrong time,' as if there were a right place and a right time to be the victim of a vicious crime.

For those who believe in an omniscient and benevolent deity who is deeply concerned for humanity, this propensity of great suffering to strike, if not always without antecedents, at least very often people whom even the strictest judges would not deem deserving of it, is something of a problem, what C.S. Lewis, in a short book of Christian apologetics, called *The Problem of Pain*.

The word *apologetics* seems to me to imply doubt or a will to believe notwithstanding opposing arguments. After all, no one writes apologetics for arithmetic, or for those things they feel sure about. It suggests a certain whistling in the wind.

I think Lewis's book, despite its fame, is very bad. I have a high regard for the man and his erudition, but his argumentation in this book strikes me as feeble and almost as dishonest. It is the work of a man who is desperate to believe something and who clutches at dialectical straws in order to be able to continue to do so.

To be fair (which does not come easily to me), he puts the case against a benevolent God quite forcefully. (It is with the benevolence, rather than with the existence, of that being that he is concerned.) There is no seeming justice to human suffering: good people are struck down and bad people can go through life like a hot knife through butter. Very few people escape suffering altogether, but a life without suffering is at least conceivable. A man may go his entire existence without illness, poverty, loss of loved ones, and so forth, and then drop dead suddenly without any previous suffering. A life of this kind is not very frequent, perhaps, but no doubt instances can be found. It is easier, of course, to find cases in which misfortune on misfortune piles on the heads of those who have done nothing extraordinary to deserve it or bring it on themselves. In my medical career, I was often struck by how there were people who had experienced far more than what might be called their fair share of suffering, as if they attracted it as a magnet attracts iron filings. How is this compatible with a loving (and just) deity?

I concede, of course, that a belief in such a being, if God can be thought of as a being, has great psychological advantages for the believer. It assures him that whatever befalls him, however horrible, there is a purpose behind it and that everything will come out right in the end. Among other proofs of this is the superior survival of religious persons in concentration camps — though people with strong and transcendent political beliefs, or faiths, also do better than those for whom such incarceration is simply unjust and meaningless.

But just as the truth of a political faith is not proved by the superior survival of believers in concentration camps, so the truth of religious faith is not proved by the psychological advantages it confers on those who have it. It may be pleasant to believe that there are fairies at the bottom of the garden, but the pleasantness of the thought has nothing to do with its truth, with whether there really *are* fairies at the bottom of the garden.

One of Lewis's ideas is that suffering is good or necessary for us, as training is necessary for a dog. We do not pretend that a puppy enjoys its house-training, but we know, because of our superior knowledge, experience and intelligence, that to house-train a dog will increase our love for it, indeed is probably a precondition of our love for it later in its life. As no one would take house-training as evidence of cruelty to a dog, in like fashion and spirit does God apply discipline to humanity — a kind of house-training on a larger scale. Among other things, it recalls us to the fact that we are not self-sufficient beings, not even a self-sufficient species, that in the midst of life we are in death, and that we owe a constant duty to our maker.

But there are naturalistic and non-religious arguments for the benefits wrought by suffering, for example it increases our psychological depths and gives us a motive for creativity. Without it, our lives would be impoverished. It is a matter of common experience that those who have known no troubles tend to shallowness. Suffering calls forth virtues such as fortitude and nobility, and when we observe suffering in others, it stimulates our compassion, kindness and selflessness.

On the other hand, suffering can just as well make people peevish, self-absorbed and oblivious to the needs of others. Which of these responses to suffering becomes uppermost in any individual depends largely, but not completely, on his previous character, and I freely admit that those of religious belief meet suffering with more dignity than those without such belief, because for them all that happens has a meaning and is not just the last in a meaningless series of one damned thing after another.

I am afraid that C.S. Lewis's attempted explanation of or justification of pain seems so much verbiage to me. There is a long discussion of Original Sin in the book, and as a metaphor for the inherent imperfection of Man it is useful. It is obvious that we are prey to conflicting desires and always will be, and that these make heaven-on-earth not only impossible but inconceivable; indeed, the very idea of heaven is incoherent so long as we retain our nature. Lewis says of the Fall — Man's degradation from a state of innocent perfection — the following, which for me does nothing to clarify the problem:

> God might have arrested this process [the Fall] by miracle: but this — to speak in somewhat irreverent metaphor — would have been to decline the problem that God had set Himself when He created the world, the problem of expressing His goodness through the total drama of a world containing free agents, in spite of, and by means of, their rebellion against Him.

But why did He set Himself the problem in the first place? Because he was bored with being the Almighty? Earlier, Lewis quoted *Revelations*: 'Thou has created all things, and for thy pleasure they are and were created.' Note that this is *for* and not *by* his pleasure: as flies to wanton boys are we to God.

The mystery of our existence (and I admit that there is one) is not explained by Lewis-type belief in God, but only pushes the mystery one stage back, not just as the result of insufficient knowledge or research, but radically and permanently. All solutions are as mysterious as the mystery they are supposed to explain. As Byron said of Coleridge, I wish he would explain his explanation.

I was in a Parisian bookshop with my French publisher who

was trying to sell the owner my books, among others. It was his first attempt to sell a book directly to a bookshop — a very good one, incidentally.

Anyhow, I thought it might increase his chance of success if I bought one or two books myself — not that I am ever really averse to doing so. Accompanying us was an Italian political philosopher, a specialist in the works of Thomas Hobbes and René Girard. It so happened that my eye fell on the latter's *Anoréxie et désir-mimétique* (Anorexia and Mimetic Desire). In a way, it was foolish of me to have bought it because Girard had written it in English, so for a native English-speaker to read a book in French translated from the English written by a Frenchman was absurd. However, the subject was one in which I had a personal interest, since my mother died of a variant of anorexia nervosa, that which occurs in old age, at the age of eighty-five. It was deeply distressing to watch it up close, and frustrating too, but not without interest if I could detach myself sufficiently.

She had had an operation for intestinal obstruction caused by adhesions secondary to an operation for cancer twenty years earlier. The operation was a success, but the wound did not heal properly, or only very slowly, because she was so thin and malnourished. For years she had starved herself but cunningly hidden the fact from me and her doctor, whom she would often consult for supposed gastrointestinal problems that frustrated her supposed desire to put on weight. It was only after her operation, when I was at her bedside in the hospital every day for the five weeks before she died, that I finally understood that she was avoiding the consumption of food by many subterfuges and on many pretexts. By then it was too late, though whether earlier recognition would have made any difference I am inclined to doubt: such was the power of her will. For the last period of her life, she would eat only a segment or two of a mandarin orange, relishing them as if they represented the finest cuisine; but any other food that was brought to her was brought at the wrong time, or of a consistency she could not swallow, or some such. The staff of the hospital were puzzled by her emaciation and seeming inability to eat; and the illogicality of it, her refusal to recognise the bogusness of her rationalisations, caused me to knot up inside, though I said nothing. Finally, I accepted that she would rather die than eat, and I reassured the staff that I would not blame them for her death. If only such superhuman self-control could have been exercised in a worthy cause, but just to remain thin! — I could not altogether conquer my own inner irritation.

I tried to think of her condition as an illness pure and simple but found that I could not.

It was of some interest to me, therefore, to read René Girard's views on the subject of anorexia, albeit that he did not refer in particular to my mother's variant of it. The Italian political philosopher assured me that this was one of Girard's minor works, the mere transcript of a lecture that he once gave.

Girard's theory is that it is mistaken to think of anorexia merely as a quirk of an individual's psychology. Given its increasing prevalence, it is, instead, an extreme form of the desire for that thinness that has become our standard of beauty and attractiveness. What starts as a desire to achieve and maintain that standard becomes detached from the standard and becomes a competition as an end in itself to be the thinnest of all. In the process, the anorexic proves her self-control to the superior of that of anyone else. The avoidance of food is the whole of her morality; and Girard, without claiming to be a psychologist, says that the anorexic does not have a failure of appetite but a distorted scale of values, in which triumph over natural appetite is the *summum bonum*. It is dangerous, because there is always the feared possibility that someone goes further than she in the search for self-control, and must therefore become ever more extreme.[42]

Anorexia, then, is an instance of mimetic desire which, together with the importance in social life of scapegoats, is Girard's main conceptual contribution to philosophical anthropology. Much of our behaviour is explicable by mimesis: we behave and desire as others do. It is only to be expected, therefore, that when the standard of beauty changes in the direction of slenderness, anorexia should increase in prevalence, especially since the ideal of beauty had been democratised in the sense that a much greater proportion of the population than formerly is now able to concern itself with such matters. Even the poor, especially young adults, are worried about their appearance — before they give up, the battle having been lost. Anorexia is both other-regarding and narcissistic. The anorexic is first worried about how she fares in competition with others, and how she appears to them, but then her competition is purely with herself, and she becomes totally self-absorbed.

---

[42] 'You can never be too thin or have too much money,' said the late Duchess of Windsor.

How does all this apply in my mother's case? My brother said that when my mother looked in the glass, she refused to see the old lady that she was by then and saw only the young woman that she had once been, all the more insistently because she had been beautiful, and no one likes to lose youthful beauty. I don't think that Girard, who died in 2015, would have considered it a refutation of his thesis that my mother had long had absolutely no social life except by telephone, and that therefore she could not have been starving herself to compete with others whom she would never meet. Human actions often escape their original intentions or purposes and become autonomous, habitual or obsessional. Originally, my mother would have wanted to preserve her youth and beauty in the eyes of others, then in her own eyes, and finally for no end at all except itself.

In the book containing Girard's lecture is the transcript of a conversation that he had with two intellectuals in Paris in 2005. One of them shrewdly asks him whether his theory, far from explaining nothing, explained too much? In other words, there was no conduct that would be incompatible with it. What explains everything explains nothing.

Notwithstanding this doubt, Girard's views are well-expressed, even in translation, and a stimulus to thought. I don't know whether the following would have interested him or seemed to him confirmatory of his theory, but when I practised briefly in South Africa, young black women who attended the local university (in those days, purely for Zulus) would ask me for medicine to make them thin. 'But you already *are* thin,' I would reply. But women who were still living in the traditional way would ask me for medicine to make them fat, which is how their husbands wanted them. 'But you already *are* fat,' I would reply.[43]

Two conceptions of beauty and attractiveness lived side by side. I, of course, sided with the slim, in the days when I gave thought to such matters. Man is the only animal capable of being dissatisfied with his own appearance.

For those of us who labour in the foothills of literature, or even on the plain that leads up to them, the figure of Anthony Trollope is curiously reassuring. No writer, I suspect, is altogether free of the hope that what he writes — or even only a sentence or phrase of it — will survive him. A *bon mot* remembered in a hundred years' time might justify an entire life.

The reason why the example of Anthony Trollope (1815–1882) is so reassuring is that he seemed to have written almost as a mechanical process rather than under the impulsion of genius or inspiration, and yet a goodly proportion of his vast output survives, at least in the sense of still being in print a century and a half, or more, after it was written. A doctor of my acquaintance said of his lucrative medico-legal reports, 'You turn the handle and the sausage comes out.' In his method of writing, Anthony Trollope would have known what he meant.

Trollope's *Autobiography*, written in the last years of his life

---

[43] In Alexander McCall Smith's series of novels about Mma Ramotswe, of the Number 1 Ladies Detective Agency, Gabarone, Botswana, the heroine is described as being 'of traditional build.'

and published in the year after his death, is a curious but very interesting document. My edition is dated 1946, and it is a salutary and to me rather alarming fact that more years have passed between 1946 and now than between Trollope's active years and 1946. This edition contains an introduction by Charles Morgan, the once esteemed and popular novelist whom I have mentioned in a previous volume of these notes. Of Trollope, Morgan writes that 'he will be mentioned in the text-books, and sometimes one or two of his many volumes will be read,' but Morgan does not make any higher claims for Trollope than Trollope makes for himself.

The very notion of textbooks of literature strikes me as odd (indeed, textbooks of *any* subject whatever will soon be a thing of the past, if they are not so already): perhaps Morgan meant that Trollope will be mentioned in *histories* of literature, although even these are not very likely to be written.

Morgan makes what seem to me to be two partially mistaken judgments. The first is that Trollope's autobiography tells us nothing about the inner man or about his emotional life. The second is that, as a writer, he lacked imagination and therefore was a prosaic, albeit amusing enough, chronicler of the life of Victorian England — or part of Victorian England.

These judgments are almost correct but nevertheless miss the significance of two important passages in Trollope's autobiography. It is true that in general the author does not write of his own emotions. His astonishing literary productivity, while he continued to hold an important and strenuous position in the Post Office, rising high in its ranks, might even be interpreted as a means of keeping his own emotions at bay. But in the autobiography, he describes, without dwelling excessively upon, a miserable childhood and miserable schooldays when — as an impoverished son of a ruined barrister — he endured bullying by and the mockery of his schoolfellows, as well as the cruelty of schoolmasters. He suffered a gross injustice at the hands of a schoolmaster, Mr Drury. 'All that,' he says, 'was forty years ago, and it burns me now as if it were yesterday.'

For a man of Trollope's reticence, this indicates passionate feeling. In fact, it is reminiscent of Dickens, for whom Trollope had only qualified admiration, who carried the scars of his childhood throughout his life. Morgan misses this, though admittedly it is Trollope's only *cri de coeur* — a flash of lightning in the dark.

Morgan says that Trollope had little or no imagination, yet some of his most famous novels in the *Chronicle of Barsetshire*, which recount English clerical life in an English cathedral city so accurately (according to churchmen themselves), were written after, and were inspired by, a very short visit to the cathedral close of Salisbury, without the author so much as having met any churchmen such as populate his books. If Trollope's account of his own life is truthful, and he seems to have been a most truthful man, his capacity for imaginative insight must have been considerable.

Incidentally, Trollope's concept of truth in autobiography is not to say all that is true, but to say nothing that is untrue. 'That I, or any man, should tell everything of himself, I hold to be impossible. Who could endure to own the doing of a mean thing? Who is there that has done none? But this I protest: — that nothing I say shall be untrue.'

Much — most — of the autobiography is a factual account of his literary activities. Trollope considered writing a job like any other[44], and it shocked people to know that he had so prosaic an attitude to his calling — if it could be called a calling after such revelations. At the end of his autobiography, he provides a list of the books he has written and the precise amount of money, down to the last penny, that he earned by them. He was able to conclude that his writings had brought him sixty-eight thousand nine hundred and thirty-nine pounds, seventeen shillings and fivepence. This certainly suggests a meticulousness of account-keeping, not to say a mania for it. Trollope thought his earnings sufficient but not princely, but for thirty-two years he earned an average of £2000 or more, the near equivalent today (though there is no exact equivalent) of £200,000. Once his career took off, he earned in some years the equivalent of £600,000. But it was not money for nothing. Sometimes he wrote as many as 10,000 words in the morning before he went off to work.

He organised postal services in the West Indies, developed the postal arrangements in Egypt and negotiated a postal treaty with the United States, travelling extensively in the process, but always writing thousands of words a day, whether in a railway carriage or on the high seas suffering from seasickness. He was also an enthusiastic, indeed fanatic, rider to hounds, which in these censorious days would be the blackest of black marks against him. Aware of accusations against the sport of cruelty, he argued that if the hunt did not

---

[44] I once shared a public platform with a sociologist who said the same of prostitution.

exist, the foxes would soon die out because they would be trapped or poisoned to extinction.

Trollope has much to say on the mechanics of writing. The writer should sit at his desk at a regular hour and count the words he has written, having previously set himself a target. But — perhaps in contradiction to this — he says:

> I have from the first felt sure that the writer, when he sits down to commence his novel, should do so, not because he has to tell a story, but because he has a story to tell.

This is not always the case. Often, the author:

> ...cudgels his brains, not always successfully, and sits down to write, not because he has something which he burns to tell, but because he feels it incumbent on him to be telling something...

Given that he also says that the author cannot afford to await inspiration, it is not easy to know how Trollope thinks he should proceed.

One passage reminded me of an incident in my own career (if that is not too grand a word for it). Speaking of literary criticism, Trollope says:

> I think it may be laid down as a golden rule in literature that there should be no intercourse at all between an author and his critic. The critic, as critic, should not know his author, nor the author, as author, his critic.

George Orwell was of precisely the same opinion, for all intercourse creates a sense of obligation inimical to truthfulness.

Once I reviewed a book by a man who was completely unknown to me, who invited me after the publication of my review to lunch at the Savoy. My review of his book had been only half-favourable, and I immediately concluded, rightly, that he was about to publish a second book which it was quite possible that I would be asked to review. It is difficult to criticise the book of a man who has bought you lunch at the Savoy, and I declined. His second book was published, and it was not as good as his first. He was later accused, and convicted, of plagiarism.

In the year in which my father was born, 1909, in the East End of London, a then well-known writer, Harold Begbie, published *Broken Earthenware*, subtitled *A Footnote to Professor James's Study in Human Nature, "The Varieties of Human Experience"*. It was dedicated to William James, the great Harvard philosopher and psychologist. In my edition of the work, one of the many later editions, is inscribed in a very clear italic hand the name of a previous owner, E.C. Thomas, Xmas 1927, of whom I can discover nothing. In the past, the great majority of people left practically no trace of themselves; soon, everyone will leave a trace. Whether this is progress, I cannot say.

James returned Begbie's compliment: 'I might as well call my book a footnote to his. I am proud of the dedication and of the references [to me] and I wish the book a great success.'

It had success, being reprinted innumerable times. Harold Begbie, who wrote science fiction as well as a personal memoir of Ernest Shackleton the Antarctic explorer and William Booth, the founder of the Salvation Army, describes in this book the conversions wrought by the latter that resulted in some of the most degraded men in London achieving respectability, then a quality not so much despised as it is today. Their lives of drunken viciousness were transformed by conversion into those of domestic tranquillity. It was not only they who were redeemed, but their long-suffering wives and cruelly neglected children. Where there had been starvation there was now nourishment; where there had been sadism there was now tenderness.

I have no reason to doubt the truth of the stories Begbie tells. He writes well and gives the impression of honesty. I know from experience that one of the few things that seemingly will move a man away from a life of crime is religious conversion. I saw this in the prison in which I worked as a doctor, and I shall return to this phenomenon in a moment.

Begbie recounts the lives of men in 1909 that were squalid beyond anything known today. I will take a single example, that of a man called John Gray. This man ran away from home to join the circus when he was fourteen, but the upshot was not at all romantic. He was ill-treated, badly fed, and overworked by his masters. By the time he reached adulthood he was a 'dipsomaniac' — an old-fashioned term. 'Turned away from circus after circus, he took at last to the cadger's life, and became what is called an "unemployable". He got drinks by performing tricks in public houses, such as, for instance, eating a cat. For what is called "a navvy's price," in other words a bob and a pot [a shilling and a pint of beer], he undertook to eat any dead cat that was brought to the bar...'

I don't think it takes much imagination to recoil at the image of this spectacle, and even more by that of the drunken hilarity of the men and women watching it.

By chance, John Gray attended an outdoor evangelical meeting and was converted. As a result, 'he married one of the women who had seen him in his rags and wretchedness, kneeling as a penitent at that first meeting. And now in his old age, he and his wife are prosperous and happy people, carrying on a good business in London, and following their religion with devotion.' (Before anyone can point it out, this story refers to an evangelical meeting before the establishment of the Salvation Army.)

Begbie refers to the moral courage of the Salvationists, who risked mockery and worse when they went into the noisome slum streets of London in the last two decades of the nineteenth century and first decade of the twentieth. From the purely rational point of view, perhaps, the uniforms and the brass bands and the doctrine itself might appear ridiculous, but it seems to me that there are situations in which there are qualities more important than reasonableness. If it takes absurdity or contradiction to make a man emerge from degradation and misery, so be it. I would not attempt to argue him out of his false beliefs, provided only that he was not trying to force them on me.

Actually, I have always had a soft spot for the Salvation Army. It dates back to my childhood when there was a

Salvationist in my school. H was a kind, gentle, smiling soul, though not in a saccharine way. He exuded a kind of spiritual calm, very different from the torment of a boy whose parents were members of another sect, the Plymouth Brethren. In a manner typical of the way we so often jump to conclusions on the basis of a single experience, I concluded that all Salvationists were as he was: and oddly enough, I have not been undeceived since, though I admit to not very extensive experience. Furthermore, when I was investigating for the pleasure of my own indignation the moral and financial dishonesty of large charities in Britain, I discovered (also to my pleasure) that the Sally Ally, as we used to call it, was by far the most honest of them, and I never see a Salvationist collecting money in the street without giving him or her something for the tin. No doubt there is another side to the question, perhaps from that of someone taking refuge for the night in one of their hostels, but all the same I cannot help but admire a movement that seeks to care for people despised, scorned or ignored by most people in society.

Begbie describes the extreme hostility to converts of their erstwhile friends and colleagues, once they converted. Whence this hostility? I suspect that it derived from the implied revelation that their own wretchedness and poverty came, at least in part, from their own conduct and of their own choice, for who does not prefer to imagine that all the problems of his existence derive from circumstances beyond his control and not at all from anything that he himself has done? Many prefer to be sunk in a state of fatalism without contentment than to risk an effort that is far from guaranteed of success. The Sally Ally, at least in the old days, offered unconditional support for those who tried but fell by the wayside, until eventually many of them succeeded.

Broken Earthenware tells the story of men — only men — degraded in common ways and who, by converting, become fine, upstanding pillars of the community. The question naturally arises, which Begbie never asks, whether the men changed because they were converted, or were converted because they had changed.

Recidivists in prison reach an age, usually some time before they are 39, when they are convicted of crimes no more. It is possible that they become better criminals — better in the technical sense of evading detection — but it is more likely that they cease to commit crimes in the first place. Whether from a reduction in levels of testosterone, or exhaustion by this way of life, they cease to burgle and rob: and I have noticed that among them are those who undergo a religious conversion at the very time they give up the life of crime.

Religious conversion allows them to give up without a sense of personal defeat, as if they had made a moral decision to give up rather than merely experienced a growing disinclination to crime because of advancing age. Religious conversion thus answers their needs perfectly.

Unfortunately, in my prison most of the conversions, especially among black prisoners, were to Islam. Moslem evangelical effort was much greater than Christian; and for the black prisoner, Islam had the advantage that conversion to it was not a surrender to British society's norms, as conversion to Christianity would have been. They wanted (I surmised) to go straight but continue to be feared at the same time. Islam squared the circle for them.

Every man who has been neither a soldier nor a sailor, said Doctor Johnson, is conscious of a sense of inferiority. I might add that so is one who has not experienced a great historical trial, such as a war or a revolution, for he does not know how he would have carried himself in one: whether he would have been found wanting in courage, humanity, etc. If you have come through such a trial with flying colours, you are set up psychologically for life.

Such a one was Bob Le Sueur. He was a youth of nineteen when the Occupation of the Channel Islands — in his case, of Jersey — started. He died, aged 102, in 2022, having not very long before published a marvellous memoir, *Growing Up Fast: An Ordinary Man's Extraordinary Life in Occupied Jersey*, which unfortunately does not seem to have had the wide circulation it deserves or attracted much notice outside Jersey itself. It is well-written and brings that baleful episode alive in the imaginations of those who did not live through it.

Ever since I visited the islands, the Occupation of them has been a subject of fascination for me. It was one of the longest occupations of any territory by the Nazis, and it was the occupation with by far the highest ratio of occupier to occupied, between one in five and one in three. To begin with, it was relatively benign, and outrages were few, but it grew harsher as time went on. Non-native inhabitants of Jersey were deported to Germany, and Spanish Republican and Russian prisoners were imported as forced labour to build the island defences against the British (many of which are still to be seen). The Normandy landings only made the hardships of the islanders worse, for the Channel Islands were bypassed by the landings, which made the importation of anything from France impossible. Autarchy, which was unviable, was thus imposed on the islands. By the end of the Occupation, the Germans, knowing the war was lost, were afraid of retribution and were in as bad a condition as the local population, perhaps even worse. Red Cross parcels had been sent, but the Germans were forbidden access to them and were afraid to break the rules concerning them for fear of later punishment.

Bob Le Sueur was a clerk in an insurance office in St Helier, the island's capital, when the Germans arrived. The manager of his office decamped to England, and he was left to manage the office himself in his absence. This he did: apparently, insurance carried on as normal throughout the Occupation, albeit that economic life in general was much reduced and by the end near-starvation was general. But the young Bob Le Sueur felt it his duty to carry on normally: it was a way to keep up morale and express a faith that the Occupation would not endure for ever. A stiff upper lip was very important to him, and for most of the population. He tells the story of an aunt of his in London, who was governess to the children of a rich family. They were at their lessons when there was an explosion in the upper part of the house.

> 'What was that?' asked one of the children.
> 'A bomb, dear,' said the governess. 'Now take your elbows off the table.'

This was both absurd and wise. It reminded me of the case of a vicious and callous multiple murderer who, on the run, was spotted by two policemen. They tried to arrest him, but he had a gun. A struggle ensued, in which one of the policemen was shot, though not dangerously injured. The policemen managed to overcome him and took him back to the station, expecting, no doubt, high praise for their bravery. Instead, the station sergeant, seeing their state of dishevelment after their struggle, said, 'You can't come in here looking like that! Straighten your ties!' Again, absurd and yet wise: an indication of high morale.

Bob Le Sueur tells of how the Germans demanded that every household fly a white flag as the Occupation started, to indicate surrender and lack of intention to attack the invaders:

> My mother had heard the news and was considering how best to raise a white flag. She was fixing a beautifully ironed white sheet to a broom, to be flown from one of the dormer windows on the top floor. But as I watched, my father intervened: "Take that down and put it back where it belongs. One of my [under]vests will be good enough." He chose a garment full of holes, and fixed it contemptuously to the broom to hang it out of the window. It was his little gesture of defiance, although I couldn't help thinking that perhaps some of Aunt Ethel's enormous bloomers might have done a better job.

Some people, decades later, criticised the population of Jersey for not having put up more resistance, but Le Sueur explains very well how this would have been impossible and very dangerous. The island measures nine miles by five, and there is no natural cover on it. The whole population was hostage and the Germans — known as *Greenfly* from the colour of their uniforms and their parasitic nature — were heavily armed. Violent resistance would have been suicidal, right to the end.

Le Sueur does not disguise the fact that there were people who denounced their neighbours to the Germans, mainly to settle accounts with them from old disputes, and so forth. The archives contain letters of denunciation, including of one Mrs Gould, who was denounced by a pair of sisters for harbouring a fugitive Russian. She was arrested, sentenced, and sent to Germany, where she was shot in Buchenwald ten months before the end of the war. That the sisters had denounced Mrs Gould became known, but after the Liberation no penalty was exacted. Under what law could it have been exacted? Having suffered five years of arbitrary rule, the people were mature enough not to demand well-merited, though legally arbitrary, vengeance.

However, there was much dangerous defiance practised, if not open resistance. When the Occupation was over, many people discovered that, unbeknown to them, their neighbours had, like them, kept radios illegally and listened to the BBC. Many people had also hidden Russian escapees at great danger to themselves and had kept their activities completely secret. Bob Le Sueur was responsible for hiding ten or twelve Russian prisoners, moving them from one safe house to another, insofar as any house could be safe.

Once, when seeking accommodation for a Russian escapee, he asked a French physiotherapist still practising on the island whether he might assist, thinking that he was the kind of man who would do so. Instead, he reacted angrily, telling Le Sueur not to be so stupid and never to ask such a thing of him again. Le Sueur was disillusioned about the man: it was only later that he discovered that at the very moment of his refusal, he was concealing a distant cousin of Le Sueur's, wanted by the Germans, and two Russian escapees, in the very building in which Le Sueur had asked for his assistance.

The stories in the memoir are so well told that it is as if one were present in person. Published when Le Sueur was 100, he must have been in his nineties when he wrote it, for he tells of how he met Prince Charles (as he then still was) in 2013. *Growing Up Fast* should be considered a classic of the genre.

I met Bob Le Sueur for the last time when I was invited to give a talk to the *Société Jersiaise* on the historiography of the Occupation. He was then in his nineties, spry, dapper, alert and with a twinkle in his eye. I felt it was really an impertinence for me to say anything on the subject in his presence, but he seemed to like what I said. He was a hero, but a modest one. I felt a vague shame in his presence: he had passed a test that I had not.

I have several times told the story of how I waited on the platform of Milton Keynes station for a train that never arrived because it had crashed further down the line at Watford, and how everyone on the platform grumbled at its lateness. It was only later that I learned that the one person killed in the crash was someone whom I knew slightly, at least by telephone. She was Ruth Holland, who was editor of the book reviews in the *British Medical Journal*, in the days when that august publication still reviewed books. I had never met her in person, but she was pleasant, polite, amusing and interesting to talk to.

I was prey to some strange and not wholly logical ideas when I learned of her death. Why, I wondered, did it have to be *she* of all the passengers, the only one to whom I had any connection, on the train to be killed? Why not someone else? I thought this as if someone *had* to die on the train, as a kind of sacrifice to the great god, Railway, but that it should not have been she. I was sure that the train was full of wastrels who would have been much less of a loss and who, moreover, were unknown to *me*. Narcissism or solipsism is never far below the surface of our minds.

The crash was, as I write this, more than twenty-six years ago, and I never go through Milton Keynes on the train — which I do surprisingly often — without thinking of Ruth Holland. If the crash had not happened, she would now have been eighty-two years old, no great age today.

Two years after her death, the *British Medical Journal* published a slim volume of her writing, titled *Wit and Fizz*. It had an introduction by the then editor of the *Journal* and, perhaps not surprisingly, it overpraised her writing. I should have done the same if asked: decency would have seemed to me to require it.

A large proportion of the book, which is only 128 pages long, is taken up by her own book reviews. She could be very funny, but one of the defects of her writing, at least in my estimation, is the irruption into it of demotic words or expressions into otherwise demure language. There is a fashion for this, especially in America, as if to demonstrate that the writer is not really the literary type at all, certainly not a snob, and in fact is one of the boys (or girls): but it jars on me. The demotic in writing should be reserved for reported speech, where it may be very funny: verbal inventiveness in the general population has not disappeared, though it may have declined since Dickens's day. In this matter I am a prude: I react to the demotic in the midst of the demure much as a maiden to a dirty joke. It makes me blush or want to.

It seems that the literary editor of the *BMJ* either chose, or was given, terrible books to review: though here once more we come across the problem of the numerator (the books reviewed in the journal) and the denominator (all the books that could have been reviewed). At any rate, what we find in Ruth Holland's review of *Reproductive Anthropology: Descent Though Women*, by Donald A.M. Gebbie, is typical of the author's amusing waspishness:

> Mr Gebbie has covered a vast amount of material. Unfortunately, in the end the material seems to have covered him.

She continues:

> He makes a brave shot at fighting back and getting control of it, but where he needs a hatchet he uses a paintbrush. Brutal culling would have improved the text much more than slapping on a garish colour supplement of unfortunate blobs of imagery like: 'The iceberg over the African continent spreads its peril far and wide;'

'Smellie[45] had opened the floodgates of pelvic menstruation'; and someone with 'large hands to boot.'

Gebbie's writing 'presumes an absolute ignorance in the reader and explains everything: "The male pelvis is not concerned with childbirth"[46]; "It is fortunate indeed that the obstetrician had no need to sex the pelvis of his or her patients as… they were all female."'

Things have become more complicated in this regard since 1983, when Ruth Holland wrote her review of a book published in 1981, and men can allegedly become women and vice versa.

Ruth Holland draws our attention to the following sentence: 'All Australian eco-wen enjoyed their sex life' and adds 'You're wondering what Australian eco-wen are, with their universally enjoyable sex lives':

> They're aborigines. Why call them eco-wen? Because Mr Gebbie is very careful of the sensibilities of those of us who are not male, not European, not industrialised, or simply not around any more. So he won't refer to Man (although, as we all know, Man embraces Woman), but Wan; not men but wen, not humans but huwans (he doesn't, as you see, give a monkey's for the jarred nerves of etymologists, or anyone who winces at monstrosities like "the White Wan's grave" "nomadic herdswen".

---

[45] William Smellie (1697–1763) was a Scottish obstetrician, famed for his new design of obstetric forceps.

[46] This, astonishingly, might be denied today by wild theorists of gender.

"Irishwen", and "wanhood")... you lop off the first syllable of a socially acceptable word like ecology, tie it to your newly minted "wen" and there you are... Sexism and racism (maybe even snobbism) are eliminated with one stroke of the pen; in the same way we eliminate the common cold by banning the word "sneeze".

This, remember, was published more than forty years ago, suggesting the gestation of Wokeness was a long one.

Apart from her death in a train crash — as a police spokesman would now put it, the consequence of being on the wrong train at the wrong time — one senses another tragedy in her life, hinted at in the introduction: namely that all her life she wanted to be a writer, especially for the theatre. Indeed, she did have three plays performed (we are not told where) early in her career. But instead of being a real writer she was reduced to writing occasional pieces and commissioning and editing the work of others. Editing is a great skill, and good editors are worth their weight in gold, but they have to be self-effacing and devoted to the glory of others. They are anonymous as far as readers are concerned; they have no glory for themselves, however much they might deserve it. I suspect that Ruth Holland was heroically self-abnegating, but possibly disappointed within. I salute her memory.

I have noticed that in provincial English charity shops — their economics are a scandal, but that is matter for another day —

that among their books for sale, among all the trashy paperback novels of which people want to disembarrass themselves while imagining that they are assisting the poor, there is almost always one work of arcane scholarship: *A History of Banking in Nineteenth Century Chile*, say, that leads one to wonder how on earth it found its way there, to account for whose presence would be a novel in itself. The reading habits of my fellow-countrymen as revealed in their donations to charity shops depress me, though of course one might look on the bright side: at least they do not treasure their trash.

Be that as it may! Recently, I went into my local Oxfam shop, and there among the trashy novels was nestling a work of obscure literary scholarship, titled *DH. Lawrence at Therroul*, by Joseph Davis, a native of that small town on the coast of New South Wales, and still a school teacher there. How it reached Oxfam in Bridgnorth I will never know.

Therroul was hardly more than a village or settlement when D.H. Lawrence and his wife stayed in it for a few weeks in 1922. The author of the book about this stay says in his preface that he himself was born in Therroul in 1956, that he is married, that he still lives in Therroul, and that he hopes that he always will. He is a fortunate man.

He was 33 when his book was published. To desire to stay where one was born from so early an age, and not from mere ignorance, is surely a happy state of mind, but one that I have never known. Not to be tortured by the idea that one is missing something important by not being somewhere other than where one is, which results in a permanent inner restlessness, is happiness indeed. The author studied English literature at Wollongong University, a city a few miles away from

Therroul, and of which the latter is now said in effect to be a suburb. Literature is all the travel Mr Davis ever needed.

When Lawrence travelled to and stayed awhile in Australia, its population was only about five and a half million, about that of Sydney today. Even now, one has the impression — which is justified — that the whole population of the country clings to the coastline as the shipwrecked would cling to a raft. The vastness of the Australian interior, its emptiness, is subliminally menacing. Australia is the most urbanised country in the world, which allows its inhabitants to put the interior out of their minds. When I went from Adelaide in the south to Darwin in the north, I thought constantly of the inland taipan, the snake with the most potent venom of any snake in the world, and though it is called the *fierce snake*, it rarely encounters humans. (For some reason, the fact that one drop of its venom is sufficient to kill 200,000 mice has always stayed with me, perhaps because of the fact's uselessness.[47])

Mr Davis's book is a small contribution to literary history. Lawrence wrote his rather strange book about Australia, *Kangaroo*, in the six weeks he spent at Therroul, at a rate of 3000 words a day, which Davis found remarkable: which it is, until one remembers that Trollope wrote twice as much for years on end, and not in a burst of creativity. Whether Lawrence will last longer than Trollope remains to be seen and of course no definitive answer can be given until the final extinction of literature.

This book is micro-history, even by the standards of literary

---

[47] I presume this was discovered by extrapolation from dilutions of the venom rather than by the slaughter of 200,000 mice.

criticism: whom Lawrence and his wife might have met in the village, where he walked, how many daytrips he took and where to, the view from his house and its surrounds, his purchases in the village shops, and so forth. And yet it is not without interest, for of this material Lawrence constructed a long book, not only about political developments in Australia (he imagined a proto-fascist movement there) but — more importantly, in the opinion of the author — the effect of the brooding immense land, which was in a sense both ancient and very new, on the character and mentality of the people. This Lawrence called 'the spirit of the place', the geographical equivalent of the zeitgeist. In fact, Lawrence's opinion of the Australians, as expressed in his letters, was not very flattering:

> The people are so crude in their feelings — and they only want to be up to date in their 'conveniences' — electric light, tramways and things like that.

Or again:

> All the outside life is so easy. But there it ends. There's nothing else. The best society in the country are shop-keepers. Nobody is better than anyone else, and it really is democratic. But it all feels so slovenly, slip-shod, rootless, and empty... I have never felt such a foreigner and I haven't one single word to say to them.

But this is summary judgment: Lawrence doesn't seem to have tried very hard to make contact with the Australians, and after all he spent only a few weeks there. On the other hand, I have myself had a conversation with an Australian — in Bangkok, I think it was — in the course of which he praised the excellence of Australian plumbing as evidence that it was the best country in the world in which to live. And I had a second cousin who lived in Australia and who had nothing but Lawrentian contempt for it because the people were so shallow and philistine. She had lived in Paris as a Bohemian and published a few verses (a line of which I remember) and was for a short time the lover of Richard Wright, author of *Notes of a Native Son*. She believed, because he died shortly after having left the American Hospital in Paris where he had been treated for amoebic dysentery, that the CIA had killed him as a Soviet sympathiser. But in those days the treatment was with the highly cardiotoxic drug, emetine hydrochloride, so he might have died of late side-effects. Somehow, my cousin was not pleased by this possibility: she wanted to believe that he had been murdered.

She was an escapee from Nazi Germany who had been for a time at the beginning of the war interned on the Isle of Man as an enemy alien, where she much enjoyed herself. After the war, she worked as an interpreter, for a time alongside Henry Kissinger. She eventually married a rich man in Australia, on condition that she could travel by ship first class to Europe every so often.

I did not agree with her about Australia, which she thought of as an absence rather than as a presence. Here I was with Lawrence when he spoke of the spirit of the place. I remember arriving in Sydney for a month's stay and smelt the flowers and heard the cockatoos and searched for dangerous spiders in the bathroom. I experienced a kind of ecstasy at its exoticism, its romance. I did not even think of the Australians as philistines, at least any more than of any other people. I admired greatly the Australian impressionist painters, whom I thought the equal of any of that genre, and who certainly conveyed 'the spirit of the place' — when the population was only 3 million. I discovered the work of Lloyd Rees, a draughtsman of extremely beautiful landscapes in pencil. An exhibition of Sydney police photographs from 1912 to 1948 was the most evocative such exhibition I have ever seem. I spent happy afternoons looking for platypuses (or is it platypi?) in a small creek. No, Australia was not the nullity that my second cousin's refusal to take an interest in it made it out to be.

If I had been a younger man, and permitted to do so, I would have stayed. D.H. Lawrence said something similar:

If I stayed here for six months I should stay here for ever.

One of the book reviews by Ruth Holland reprinted in her little book, *Wit and Fizz*, was laudatory rather than cutting or scathing. Its title was *Mad Lucas: The Strange Story of Victorian England's Most Famous Hermit*, by Richard Whitmore. And indeed, it is an admirable book, from more than one point of view.

Richard Whitmore was for many years a minor celebrity in England, though he was completely unknown to me, because he read the news on BBC television — which I never watched. He must have been recognised everywhere he went, but there is evidence from my copy of his book that he was not unduly impressed by his own fame, nor was he star-struck by himself.

In the first place, he has lived in the town of Hitchin in Hertfordshire all his life and now, at ninety-one, still lives there. He has written several books of local history, and I do not think that the writing of books of local history is an activity to which narcissistic celebrities are much given.

In the second place, laid in my copy of the book is a letter from him to a correspondent who wrote to him when he was still at the BBC and at the height of his fame. It is addressed to a Mrs Wintle who lived, or lives, in Norfolk. It is hand-written and thanks her for kind comments on his book, adding that it is good to know that his book about Mad Lucas, who lived in Hitchin, had been read as far afield as Norfolk. These are not the words of a man who expects, or wants, world-fame from his historical research, and who may therefore be presumed to have carried them out for their own sake, simply because he found the subject interesting and possibly for the glory of his beloved town. This is not to say that his research was not arduous or time-consuming, and in his acknowledgments, he thanks the staff of many libraries and also the North Hertfordshire District Council for having agreed to publish his book, as well as the latter's Museum Services Sub-committee and its chairman, Philip MacCormack. The book is dated 1984, which hardly counts as pre-history, yet the acknowledgments seem to come from a distant age, more civilised or refined than our own, when a district council was still capable of worthwhile cultural patronage.

Third, there is Mr Whitmore's handwriting itself. There is

no art to find the mind's construction in the hand, perhaps[48], but nevertheless I should guess from it that the man was not a flamboyant type, but modest without being altogether self-effacing. This impression is strengthened by the fact that, though the letter is on BBC Television notepaper, the envelope, which is laid in with the book, is addressed in Mr Whitmore's hand also, and not typed by some minion. I doubt whether today anyone as famous as was he would deign to go to this trouble. It would be a case of *lèse-célébrité* to do so.

All this aside, his book, published, and well-published too, by North Hertfordshire District Council, is extremely interesting, especially to a doctor. Its subject, James Lucas (1813–1874), was a wealthy man who lived in filth and squalor for several decades in his ancestral home that was crumbling around him by neglect. He was eccentric even in his youth, riding out in a completely yellow outfit of an abnormal cut, his horse being caparisoned in the same colour. He was odd not in order to attract notice to himself, but simply because it never occurred to him to do otherwise than he did. What was bizarre to others was normal to him.

The primordial event in his life was the death of his mother. He insisted on keeping her corpse in the house and gave it up for interment only when forced to do so. Otherwise, he would have kept it forever, and certainly he preserved his mother's bedroom in precisely the state it was when she died; her bed was made and the sheet turned back, and her books of religious poetry were still on the bedside table when James Lucas in turn died. By then, the house was nearly a ruin and

---

[48] Hand here means handwriting, of course.

uninhabitable, except by him. When he died, he had dressed for more than twenty years only in a blanket, and he slept in the cinders of the fire that he kept going at all times. He subsisted only on bread, milk and cheese, with an occasional herring, and he never washed. He was indescribably filthy; he never cut his hair, beard or fingernails, which were three inches long. He never left the house and barred and bolted all the windows so that no one could enter. He believed that his brother was trying to kill him; he was paranoid about him but possibly had a bad conscience with regard to him, for by continuing to live in the house he was depriving him of part of his rightful inheritance.

His preservation of his mother's room exactly as it was, except for the inevitable ravages of time, is reminiscent of Miss Havisham[49], and indeed James Lucas has his tiny place in literary history, namely the visit that Charles Dickens paid him in 1861. He, James Lucas, had become famous locally for his extraordinary way of life, and attracted many visitors who desired to stare at and talk to him. Although hermetically sealed in his house, he was delighted to have such visitors and was very kindly disposed towards children, especially little girls, whose hands he would kiss through the bars of his windows, and to whom he gave money and sweets. He was generous to passing tramps, giving them money and gin according to whether they were, in order of favour, Roman Catholic, Anglican or Non-conformist. Knowing this, tramps would claim to be Roman Catholic in order to obtain the maximum from him, but he would test them to discover

---

[49] Charles Dickens, *Great Expectations*.

whether they really were Catholic or only pretending to be. He was a Jacobite to the extent of believing Queen Victoria was a usurper of the throne and refused to accept or sign any document bearing her effigy on it, for example with a postage or revenue stamp. This meant that he could not conduct any business, and he gave power of attorney to his bank to avoid compromising his principles.

Dickens detested Mad Lucas and thought it very wrong of him to live as he did when he could have been a useful member of society. He wrote a long, semi-fictional account of his visit, *Tom Tiddler's Ground*, in which the great author described Lucas's way of life and physical appearance and living conditions with great exactness but with no sympathy whatever, and he transcribed his exchanges with him.

Richard Whitmore suggests that Mad Lucas was a paranoid schizophrenic, but I think he was too articulate for that. He seems in his conversation with Dickens to have got the better of him, and in my experience, it is impossible to have a coherent conversation with genuine madmen who live in squalor because of their schizophrenia. Their thoughts are disordered, and what they say is so fractured that it is impossible to follow their meaning. For some reason, such people in Paris often choose the Réamur-Sebastopol Métro station for their day residence; they mutter to themselves, talk to invisible interlocutors and make the passenger tunnels smell. They would not be able to get the better of a great author.

James Lucas's brother tried to get him committed as a lunatic to an asylum, but he failed. The Commission in Lunacy, as it was then called, thought that Lucas, though extremely peculiar, posed no threat to himself or to others. Whitmore has a brief but highly intelligent discussion of the rights of the mad versus the rights of the rest of society, a question that is still unresolved because it is unresolvable. Does the freedom of the mad but harmless to lead their lives as they choose outweigh the distress that they cause to those who hear and smell them as they pass by? No doubt it is a matter of degree; and where there are matters of degree, there are no definitive answers.

After Lucas died (the house had had to be broken into to remove him as he was dying), his body was cleaned up:

> It was as if the covering of soot and grease had preserved him from age. His cleansed skin had the pure, white, smooth alabaster quality of a boy. His hands, the long nails trimmed, were small and delicate like those of a woman. His body was muscular and well-proportioned... In death his face was serene, indeed handsome; that of a distinguished and intellectual man of high birth... Esther Parker, who helped to lay him out, commented afterwards, 'A more beautiful corpse I have never seen.'

Thirty years earlier, Dickens had put the words, 'He'd make a lovely corpse' in the mouth of the drunken slatternly nurse, Mrs Gamp.

Richard Whitmore, the author of the book on Mad Lucas,

also wrote an excellent and judicious biography of Reginald Hine, another figure who intrigues me. Hine, who died in the year of my birth, though a few months before that auspicious event, was a solicitor who achieved some fame as a local historian, also of the town of Hitchin. The biography is a model of its kind, sympathetic without hagiography, and of a length suitable to its subject. It is very well-written and produced, and deserves to be more widely known, for Reginald L. Hine was a very interesting and largely admirable man, though not without defect that led him to mildly disreputable professional conduct and ultimately to his tragic downfall and ruin.

In 1945, Hine published his *Confessions of an Un-Common Attorney*, a memoir that is not easy to classify, but delightful in the sense of being full of delight, a pudding with many plums. It had me laughing more than once, but also on occasion very moved.

Hine was by no means an enthusiastic lawyer. He chose the law because, as the youngest son of a prosperous tenant farmer who was an important figure on Hitchin council, he had to choose to do something. He entered the law not by university, but as a kind of apprentice, an articled clerk for a firm of lawyers that had been founded in the seventeenth century and whose premises in Hitchin dated from then. He was a clerk for thirty years, and it was not until he was fifty that, reluctantly, he qualified as a solicitor. This was not because he lacked ability, but because he was far more interested in local history than in the law, and documents dating back centuries were to be found in the offices of his firm. He had the instincts of an archivist, antiquary, bibliophile, chronicler and historian; and, astonishingly and fortunately for posterity, the senior partner of the firm, William Onslow Times, was sympathetic and understanding, and was content to pay him full time wages for half-time work, the other half of his time dedicated to his historical research which resulted in a two volume, thousand-page work, *The History of Hitchin*, and what is regarded as his masterpiece, *Hitchin Worthies*.

Hine had also taken the wise precaution of marrying the daughter of a wealthy ship-owner, which no doubt explains the presence of a Canaletto on his office wall, and his ability to collect books of the kind and antiquity that only very rich men can buy.

Hine was a man after my own heart, though I am without either his flamboyance or his erudition. I could certainly not, as he could, interpret mediaeval documents. His greatest find, perhaps, was the surrender document of Hitchin Priory to Henry VIII during the Dissolution of the Monasteries in 1539. But he delighted in small details that he thought (rightly) illuminated wider history, as well as in the sheer variability of human beings. He was sympathetic to all religions, even when they were in conflict with one another, and though he was some kind of believer, he could not commit himself to any one sect. His father's family was Methodist, his mother's Anglican.

I surmise that Hine was a man of strong emotion but one who was reluctant to express it in person to others. He hid behind his arcane erudition and sense of humour. When asked by the novelist Ursula Bloom to intercede on behalf of her father, an errant parson who had been constrained by his extramarital affairs with women to resign from the Church of England clergy, to ask for the return of his clerical licence, he wrote to the Archbishop of Canterbury, who replied that the record of the parson, which 'made distressing reading', precluded it. Hine thought of a reply, which he did not send:

> Your Grace, we grieve to learn that you should despair of our client's spiritual condition and that you should entertain little hope of a genuine repentance. All we can say to convince you is that, whereas in our client's prime he kept five concubines, now at the age of eighty he has reduced the number to two. Is there not here reasonable ground for hope?

Hine enjoyed absurdity. Among the ancient documents, title deeds and so forth, that he found in the old cupboards of his employer's offices, including a letter from the poet Andrew Marvell, in which he complained that no one could expect promotion, spiritual or temporal, without flattery of the King's[50] mistress, the Duchess of Cleveland, was the draft of a bill in Parliament to forbid any woman 'to impose upon, seduce or betray into Matrimony any of His Majesty's subjects by means of scent, paint, cosmetic washes, artificial teeth, Spanish wool, iron stays, hoops, high-heeled shoes, or bolstered hips.' The idea of seduction by false teeth will amuse me always, even (I hope) on my deathbed.

Hine pays tribute to a research assistant, clearly a highly educated man, whom he employed for a time who 'was willing to work for me, and willing to write to me, but on no account would he meet me.' He discovered why this was one day,

---

[50] Charles II

when he was pointed out to him by someone who knew him. 'He was the ugliest man I have ever seen.' Hine describes his face in some detail and then continues:

'Ugly as sin,' you would say. But you would be wrong. In fact, the man was a saint. He worked himself to the bone. He lived on nothing a week. And all the money he made (it was little, because he never sent in a bill, and took like a beggar whatever you chose to give him), all that little was handed in to the Children's Hospital.

Then his assistant went quiet:

Three months later all my notes and queries were returned to me, with a business letter from him broken off in the middle — not a word about himself — and a screed from [his] landlady to inform me that her lodger had been [readmitted] to the Children's Hospital and there had died. God rest his soul, and God forbid that there should be any resurrection of his body.

This is written with real feeling.

In 1920, a barrister called Edward Smithson, who had retired to Hitchin, where he occupied himself by writing books 'proving' that William Shakespeare, the writer of the plays, was really Francis Bacon, the philosopher, consulted him, a fellow-writer, about his writer's block. Hine said to him, 'Don't worry... I just go on in the blind faith that somehow the confounded sentence will come out right in the end.' Smithson left his office and shot himself dead a few hours later.

Twenty-one years after that, Hine, facing disgrace for a minor and probably well-intentioned infringement of professional etiquette, jumped in front of a train at Hitchin Station, in full view of other passengers.

It is perhaps ironic that he had previously asserted that the study of history endues us 'with understanding, patience and equanimity; and these are qualities of incalculable value in the conduct of human affairs.'

Four doors away from where I write this lived Richard Baxter. On the whitewashed wall of this tiny half-timbered cottage are inscribed the words, 'In this house lived the learned and eloquent Richard Baxter, 1640–1641.' For years, I read the word 'eloquent' as 'elegant', though the house seems hardly commodious enough for elegance of any kind (though the current occupant is a snappy dresser). I suppose I prefer the quality of elegance to that of eloquence, which I mistrust. Both, perhaps, are misleading, but eloquence is more dangerously misleading.

Strangers who pass the house wonder, and are apt to ask, who Richard Baxter was. The answer is both simple and complex. He was born in 1615 and died in 1691. He was a clergyman who navigated the choppy waters between High Church Anglicanism and extreme Puritanism and kept his head (literally) through the turbulent years of the Civil War and Commonwealth. He was a prolific writer on religious subjects, and I once read that he published more than any other writer in English, at least until the advent of the typewriter.

Apparently, he didn't think much of the people of my town, whom he regarded as an impious drunken rabble. It is certainly true that within a radius of a hundred yards of my house there are still to be found a large number of drinking establishments, for example the Bear, the Harp, the Jewel of the Severn, the Golden Lion, the King's Head, and the Crown, not to mention the Atrium, The Jeroboam, and the Royle. Within crawling or staggering distance are the George, the Old Castle, the Shakespeare, the White Lion, the Black Boy (which advertises itself as a day-care centre for husbands), the Brandon Arms, the New Inn, the Friars, the Falcon and the Vines — and I apologise if I have missed one or two. The Swan, alas, seems to have sung its last song; but even this truncated list suggests that there is one drinking establishment for every 600 inhabitants of the town, including women and children.

There is therefore no reason for anyone in our town to suffer from delirium tremens as a result of severance from alcohol, though it must be said that public drunkenness has declined somewhat of late, perhaps because of inflation. Surprisingly enough, each of the named establishments has its own character and clientele: one for drug purchase, for example, one for betting and drinking oneself to death, another for the kind of people who keep gun dogs, and so forth.

But back to Richard Baxter and sobriety. The portrait of him suggests a severe man for whom levity was a sin: we were not placed on this earth merely to laugh, not even for part of the time. When he removed himself to a nearby, much larger town, he created something of a public disturbance there by maintaining that unbaptised babies who died went straight to Hell, which does not, to a modern sensibility, do much honour to God's mercy, all the more so as the doctrine was enunciated at a time of much infant death.

It comes as rather a surprise then, to read his long sermon published as a short book, *The Cure for Depression and Excessive Sorrow*. By then he was in his sixties and had moderated his views somewhat, for one might have supposed that for Baxter, no sorrow could have been excessive where it was the product of guilt and where everyone was a sinner *ex officio*: instead of which Baxter calls for moderation in breast-beating. He came to regard excessive self-reproach almost as blasphemous, insofar as it appears to be a denial of the infinite forgiveness of our sins opened to us as a possibility by God's self-sacrifice (I have never really understood the doctrine).

Baxter says, 'Sorrow is excessive when it is fed by a mistaken cause.' He says, 'All is too much where none is due, and great sorrow is too much when the cause requireth but less.'

> If a man thinketh that somewhat [something] is a duty, which is no duty, and then sorrows for omitting it, such sorrow is all too much, because it is undue, and caused by error.

There are some, he says, who feel guilt because they do not think of God all the time but go about their daily business without Him uppermost in their minds. But 'superstition always breeds such sorrows, when men make themselves religious duties which God never made them, and then come short in their performance of them.'

> Many fearful Christians are troubled about every meal
> that they eat, about their clothes, their thoughts, and
> words, thinking or fearing that all is sinful which is lawful,
> and that unavoidable infinities are heinous sins.

There is, of course, a grandiosity in this overgrowth of
conscience, and there is a tendency to it still, though it has
been secularised. Everything that we do is invested with a deep
moral significance; we cannot so much as eat a biscuit or buy
a new shirt without supposedly harming the planet, and it is
reassuring to know that we are so very important, even if it is
only in doing harm. But, says Baxter:

> Sorrow is excessive when it hurteth or overwhelmeth
> nature itself, and destroyeth bodily health or
> understanding... God will have mercy and not sacrifice;
> and he that would not have us kill or hurt our neighbour
> on pretence of religion, would not have us destroy or hurt
> ourselves, being bound to love our neighbours as
> ourselves.

The sermon, in effect, is a prolonged call to moderation and
that most neglected of all the senses, that of proportion:

> When sorrow [meaning guilt] swalloweth up a sinner, it
> is excessive, and to be restrained.

This is because:

> The passion of grief and trouble of mind do oft overthrow the sober and sound use of reason, so that a man's judgment is corrupted and perverted by it, and it is not in that case to be trusted...You may as easily keep the leaves of trees in quietness and order in a blustering wind as the thoughts of one in troubling passion.

We should remember always (if we are Christian, which I am not) that 'where sin aboundeth, grace super-aboundeth.' This doctrine has its dangers, for if everything can be forgiven on repentance, what matter what we do? But I can at least rejoice that my neighbour of nearly four centuries ago was, or at least became, no fanatic.

As it happens, while reading Baxter, I also leafed through my 1698 folio of the *Book of Common Prayer*, and my eye fell on the following:

> Show yourselves joyful unto the Lord, all you lands; sing, rejoice and give thanks.
> Praise the Lord upon the harp: sing to the harp with a psalm of thanksgiving.
> With trumpets also and shawms: O show yourself joyful before the Lord the King.

Baxter would have agreed, at least in the later stages of his life.

Alas, my edition of *The Cure for Depression and Excessive Sorrow* is the last, not the first, and is a reprint by an American evangelical press, dating from 2015. It replaced Baxter's quotations from the Authorised (King James) version of the Bible by the English Standard version, copyright Good News

Publishers. Thus:

> So that contrariwise ye ought rather to forgive him, and comfort him, lest perhaps such a one should be swallowed up with overmuch sorrow...

becomes:

> So you should rather turn to forgive and comfort him, or he may be overwhelmed by excessive sorrow...

and:

> It is reported commonly that there is fornication among you...

becomes:

> It is actually reported that there is sexual immorality among you...

Good heavens! Who would have thought it?

Twelve years before Richard Baxter came to live in my town, the ship, the *Vasa*, sank two hours into its maiden voyage in the waters off Stockholm. For 330 years, the Swedish king's flagship lay on the bottom of the sea, its precise location having been forgotten, though efforts to salvage it continued for several decades after it sank, some of them partially successful, for some of the ship's guns were recovered using the primitive methods of the time.

The *Vasa* was found again in 1956 and lifted from its muddy bed in 1961. On a visit to Sweden with my father in 1962, who was on business, I saw it in its temporary museum before it had been fully restored. It was impressive even then, but no one called it a work of art, as they do now.

I hadn't thought about the *Vasa* for more than sixty years when I happened upon a book about its recovery of the title *Vasa: The King's Ship*, by a commander of the Royal Swedish Navy, Bengt Ohrelius. It is a short book, and I presume it was well-written, for it reads well in English, and it is difficult to turn an ill-written book in one language into a well-written one in another.

Vasa was published in 1962, the year of my visit, and as one might expect of a writer who was both a professional sailor and a marine archaeologist, it is strong on technical detail. The salvage of the ship was indeed a technical feat, and one comes away with admiration for the dedication, skill, bravery and ingenuity with which it was performed. At over a hundred feet below the sea's surface, and sunk in mud, the divers had to work in complete darkness, for even the most powerful lamps of the time could not penetrate the murk in which the *Vasa* lay.

But there were two other things in the book that impressed themselves on me perhaps even more.

The first was the account of the official inquiry into the disaster that immediately followed. Commander Ohrelius's account of that inquiry is strongly reminiscent of any such inquiry in Britain today, in which the aim was not so much to find out what happened as to find someone to blame, preferably someone low in the hierarchy. Indeed, the general principle of such inquiries — including coroner's inquests — is to fix blame on the lowest possible person in the hierarchy on whom it can plausibly be fixed, usually because he has failed to carry out some detail of official procedure. If procedure were followed, there would never be any disasters.

The *Vasa* capsized in a mere puff of wind, so something must have been wrong with it. Perhaps the design was wrong, perhaps it was overloaded, perhaps the ballast was wrongly placed, perhaps the rigging was wrong for the conditions. The master of ordnance was responsible for the placement and securing of the guns, sixty-four of them, that each weighed two tons. But he told the inquiry that they had been properly lashed, therefore the loss of the ship had nothing to do with him, or them. He thought the ship was top-heavy, but that was not part of his responsibility.

The man in charge of the rigging was accused of not having drawn attention to the top-heaviness of the *Vasa*, but he said he was concerned only with the rigging, and that he knew nothing of boat building. He said he never thought a ship could capsize so quickly but that he had no idea why it did.

The captain said that he had reported to the admiral that the ship was top-heavy and had conducted tests before its maiden voyage. He had had thirty men run from side to side on the ship three times, and each time the ship had listed a little more. If he had continued the test, he said, the ship would have gone right over, but the admiral had ordered him to stop. He, the admiral, said that the captain was carrying too much ballast but also that the ship builder (who conveniently was now dead) had built ships before and they had always been all right.

The man who had completed the building of the ship after the original builder's death, when asked why he had built it as he had, said that he was following the instructions of the previous builder. The builder's brother was asked about the design and replied that it had had the full approval of the King. At this point, further enquiry became too inconvenient to pursue.

So in the end the inquiry came to no conclusion, since any conclusion might have suggested that the admiral and the King were to blame, largely if not completely.

As is so often the case with calamities, responsibility was probably dispersed. The design was bad, warnings were ignored, ultimate authority could not be challenged and had to be protected. It was all too familiar to me from present practice.

The second thing that impressed me, however, was how much in other respects our mentality has changed. Life on board the *Vasa*, as on all ships at the time, was almost unimaginably hard. The sailors were cramped in their quarters, no doubt dirty and stinking, they were ill-fed and ill-clothed, susceptible not only to illness but to draconian and cruel discipline and punishment. Building a ship of the *Vasa*'s proportions, incidentally, was a nationwide effort (Stockholm of the time had a population of only 10,000, but it was far the largest city in the country).

And yet the extent, expense and beauty of the ship's decoration was astonishing. Clearly the Swedes of the time, or perhaps I should say those with power in Sweden, did not have a purely utilitarian outlook. The magnificent and elaborate wood-carving of the stern could not have made any physical difference to the fighting capability of the ship which, after all, was expected to take part in hazardous activities beyond that of merely going to sea, which was hazardous enough. Yet it put to sea with decoration that might not have disgraced a cathedral. As if this were not enough, it was built at a time of financial crisis, when the state could not pay its debts and sailors went unpaid and mutinied at the risk of death. All the same, an intense effort went into this decoration, almost as if it had been an end in itself. The question of raw utility must have been alien to those who ordered the ship, though perhaps they thought that the display of magnificence was essential to morale and the maintenance of their power. Perhaps, too, such magnificence was intended to impress an enemy richer and more powerful than Sweden. Thus, the decoration had its utility, perhaps, though not in the usual utilitarian sense.

Was this indifference to utilitarian utility a good thing or a bad?

For most people in Europe, the name *Ursula* would, at least for now, conjure up Ursula von der Leyen, the present President of the European Commission. Before that, it might have meant St Ursula, the virgin martyr of Cologne of the fourth century who was born in Cornwall. Nowadays, of course, girls go to much more trouble to lose than to defend their virginity. The headmistress of a primary school, the wife of a Church of

England vicar of the old type, once told me that a girl of about eight came crying to her because she had been mocked by other children for being a virgin. The headmistress asked her what she meant by 'virgin', to which she replied, 'I don't know, but I know that it's something horrible.'

Ursula was also the name of a very popular English romantic novelist of the first half of the twentieth century, Ursula Bloom. She once threatened to sue Reginald Hine, who has made an appearance in this book a few pages back, for libel. She had been his friend and client, but she was angered when she read the following passage in his memoir, *The Un-Common Attorney*:

> I have one client — the novelist Ursula Bloom — who on the conclusion of a [legal] matter sends me an appreciation, or valediction, in verse. But then, she is a law unto herself, for, often, the original instructions will come tripping along in witty, well-turned couplets, and she waits for a witty reply. In the wear and tear of office life, it can be rather trying. But, with the assistance of nimble-minded clerks, and with the Rhymer's Lexicon by Loring[51] at my elbow, I will do my best; and when the bill goes in, the gracious lady (if she ever looks at a bill) will find the special item: 'To mental strain in replying to your letters in verse.'

Ursula Bloom objected to the words 'if she ever looks at a bill,' for she believed, or claimed to believe, that they implied that

---

[51] Andrew Loring (1858–1929), *The Rhymer's Lexicon*, 2nd ed. 1920

she did not pay her bills. I think a more reasonable interpretation would have been that she was too grand to occupy herself with such trifling affairs and passed them on to a minion to deal with them, simply paying whatever was asked without further examination on her part. After all, she wrote some 500 books and made a fortune from them; she must have been a formidably busy person.

She prevailed, however. The case never went to court, and she settled for the removal of the offending words in all future editions (surprisingly, several were called for). Richard Whitmore, in his aforementioned and excellent biography of Hine suggests that the real reason for her annoyance was what Hine wrote about her father, the Reverend Harvey Bloom, and also the fact that she was herself thinking of writing a biography of him which Hine to some extent forestalled, in the process revealing to the public what would be the most interesting, which is to say salacious, details of his life.

I don't think this is quite right. Ursula Bloom did indeed publish a biograph of her father, titled *Parson Extraordinary*, but only in 1963, fourteen years after Hine's death. She was clearly not a slow writer, and *Parson Extraordinary* would not have taken even a slow writer fourteen years to complete. I think she was probably upset by Hine's jocular depiction of the father's extra-marital affairs, as if they were the most important aspect of his whole life.

In fact, he was a very distinguished archivist (perhaps Hine sensed a rival, for like Hine, Bloom was a keen naturalist). Bloom was but two years dead when Hine published his memoir, which Hine had written several years earlier while Bloom was still alive, and therefore capable of suing him for libel.

In her book, Ursula Bloom portrays her father as a brilliant and charming, but an impulsive and foolish, man. He had two passions: one for ancient documents and the other for flirtation, usually with women who had missed the boat where marriage was concerned. His daughter makes his affairs sound rather innocent, certainly not wildly erotic, but which were nevertheless sufficient to alienate his long-suffering wife, Ursula Bloom's mother. He spent a lot of time away from home, supposedly to work in libraries, but often to continue his flirtations. They were sufficient to ruin his reputation.

The biography depicts a man of too many parts to use his brilliant gifts to maximum advantage. He spread himself too thin to achieve lasting fame, though like his daughter he wrote many books, mainly of an erudite but very recherché kind. Although more than once offered preferment in the Church of England — before his extra-marital activities were known to the hierarchy — he preferred to remain a country parson, and in all his parishes he evinced a very real and practical compassion for the poor, by whom he was loved in return, for example staying all night by a bedside to comfort the dying. He was aware of the need for social reform such as the provision of medical and above all sanitary services, but at the same time he enjoyed the life of the local gentry: their garden, house and tennis parties. He was an excellent teacher.

His wife, however, could tolerate his philandering no more and left him with their two children, Ursula and brother Joscelyn. They went to live in lodgings, though Mrs Bloom loved her husband to the last — which is more tragic than if she had come to hate him. And although Ursula was very angry with her father for having caused the break-up of the family, she was later reconciled with him, and her book, far from being bitter, is clearly affectionate and admirative. It gives a very different impression of him from Hine's, who depicts him as an insouciant Don Juan bicycling round his parish in search of lovers.

There is a deeply affecting photograph of Ursula's mother, taken in 1915, shortly before her death. She is dressed as an Edwardian lady, but if pallor could shine, it shines from this photograph. It is as if posing for the photograph were her last, supreme effort before her death.

The Reverend Bloom remarried a woman with whom he had a long-standing affair that finally wrecked his marriage. She was in every way the inferior of his wife (which is why, perhaps, he preferred her). His wife was an accomplished woman who could help him in his literary endeavours and was far more attractive physically than his second wife. His second wife was never beautiful, and towards the end of her life was completely bald. She wore a black wig that often slid at an angle and fell off. She had no conversation, and Ursula could not see whatever it was that her father saw in her. Perhaps her inferiority and dependence might have put him at his ease; in any case, Ursula felt not bitterness towards, but an evident compassion for her.

Ursula's father, who in his eighties was living in the country, went to London during the Blitz (that killed 50,000 civilians) because he was curious to see the bombs fall. He found it aesthetically a fine sight. He would stroll in the street during a bombing raid despite a policeman's advice that he should take shelter (evidently, it was easier to find a policeman during the Blitz in London than it would be today).

He was an expert on, among other things, harvest spiders, publishing papers on that subject, as well as the licensed doctors of London during the reign of Henry VIII, a list of whose names he published. He is even more forgotten than his daughter.

It would be an interesting experiment to walk down a busy street in London and inquire of passers-by whether they had ever heard of Wilfrid Wilson Gibson (1878–1962). I think you could probably ask at least a thousand before you found anyone who had heard of him, and until comparatively recently I hadn't either, not in fact until I bought a slender and fragile book, or booklet, by him, published in 1915. In his time, however, he was well-known, insofar as poets could be well-known. His reputation was soon eclipsed, however, by that of modernists such as T.S. Eliot. Whether the modernists did the eclipsing by means of their own propaganda, I cannot say; it suffices that poetry that bore its meaning on its sleeve, as it were, as Gibson's did, went out of fashion, perhaps because it gave no employment to literary critics.

Gibson was one of the first poets (first in time, that is) of the Great War. He was not explicitly anti-war in any political sense, at least not in 1915, but I don't think that anyone could conclude after reading him that he thought that the war was an explosion of patriotism, gallantry and individual heroism. He wrote from the ordinary soldier's point of view and did not equivocate about his suffering. His lines are heartfelt.

Gibson was a Northumberland man, and though he never lived there after his youth, that county's landscape, with its pastel northern skies, marked him for life, and he frequently returned to it in his imagination.

The book, or booklet, by means of which I first learned of him bore the simple title, *Battle*. In a way it is remarkable that anything so contrary to the exalted patriotism of the time could have been published in the midst of so total and all-encompassing a conflict. There is nothing pro-British or anti-German in it, no flag-wagging, or anything of that nature. There is only tragedy and suffering; and the nearest to heroism expressed is an admirable stoicism, a stoicism that, for good or evil, could hardly be a mass phenomenon today. It is for good because it would not now be conceivable to throw away the lives of millions of young men in the same way: each person values his own life too highly for that to be possible. On the other hand, it is for evil because it means that there is and could be no cause for anyone that is higher than himself, and for which he would sacrifice himself, which bespeaks an absence of transcendent meaning to life.

The prospect of death to a soldier in the trenches is no more than a matter of regret rather than something to make a fuss over. A soldier in a trench warms himself by a brazier:

> I sit beside the brazier's glow,
> And drowsing in the heat,
> I dream of daffodils that blow,
> And lambs that frisk and bleat…
>
> Next year the daffodils will blow

And lambs will frisk and bleat;
But I'll not feel the brazier's glow,
Nor any cold or heat.

Nostalgia becomes tragedy in a few simple words. How foolish seem our daily troubles or irritations by comparison! How spoilt we are! I feel ashamed so often to work myself up into a fury over nothing. Why does it take the proximity of death to appreciate the simple glories of existence?

When death is daily to be expected, it is no great thing, either in others or in oneself. Gibson writes — mostly — through the eyes of the ordinary soldier. Here, he describes breakfast in the trenches:

We ate our breakfast lying on our backs,
Because the shells were screeching overhead...

The narrator has a bet, with a bit of bacon as the stake, on the result of a football match between Hull and Halifax (this was in the days when footballers were genuine local proletarian heroes and not hired, prodigiously paid mercenaries):

Ginger raised his head
And cursed, and took the bet; and dropt back dead.
We ate our breakfast lying on our backs,
Because the shells were screeching overhead.

To raise one's head in the trenches was, of course, to court immediate death by sniper, which is what Ginger had done: but when it happened, life had — for a time — to continue.

For the inhabitants of Flanders' warscape, the war was as terrible as for the soldiers. Here is described the total destruction of a farmhouse:

> So suddenly her life
> Had crashed about that grey old country wife…

She wanders, bewildered and confused on the churned-up ground:

> New-widowed and bereft
> Of her five sons, she clung to what was left,
> Still hugging all she'd got –
> A toy gun and a copper coffee pot.

This, you may think, must be an eye-witness account: but not at all. Gibson did eventually manage to join up (he was turned down several times on medical grounds) but never left England and worked for the army only as a bureaucrat. His war poems were the product of pure hearsay from soldiers on leave and the workings of his own imagination. Their immediacy is all the more remarkable for that.

This war to end all wars soon brought forth another, which Gibson lived to see, in a sense closer-up than the first, for he lived through the Blitz. By then, Gibson was well into his literary eclipse, and his verse seemed terminally old-fashioned. Once again, though, he resorted to his imagination, and no doubt to verbatim report. In a book of the same dimensions as *Battle*, titled *The Alert*, published in 1941, he writes through the eyes of a soldier, wounded and dying in the Libyan desert:

As wounded, on the Libyan sand he lies...
Above him seems to rise
Kindled by sunset, all about it flying
Jackdaws with gilded wings and burnished plume;
And in his ears as he is dying
Their homely cawing and the old careless chimes
Recall the innocent days
Of war-unshadowed times;
And once again with other boys he plays
Happily on the green slopes of the Sale
In the late summer light
While from the Abbey tower resounds the peal
Of ringers practising on Thursday nights.

One can only hope that this is an accurate foreshadowing of one's own death, the remembrance of happy, innocent times.

The passage of a book from the library of Corpus Christi College, Oxford, to the shelves of Oxfam in Bridgnorth, Shropshire, must have been a strange and perhaps an interesting one, and it was undertaken by my copy of *Keeling's Letters & Recollections*, edited by E.T., and with an introduction by H.G. Wells, published in 1918. When I saw the title on the spine, I felt a slight guilt that I had not the faintest idea who Keeling was: the title seemed to imply that I ought to have known. My curiosity was aroused.

The bookplate intrigued me also. It said in Latin that this book was bequeathed to Corpus Christi College by Robertus

Carolus Kirkwood Ensor, Knight Bachelor, who was fellow of the college from 1937 to 1946 and honorary fellow from 1953 to 1958 (the year of his death aged 81).

Robert Charles Kirkwood (R.C.K.) Ensor was an academic historian best known for his volume in the Oxford History of England, *England 1870–1914*, the best-selling book in the series and still in print. He was not otherwise prolific.

The inside pastedown of the book bore two small but conspicuous stamps: *Deleted by order of the Library Committee*, presumably of Corpus Christi College. The word *deleted* struck me as slightly unpleasant, as if there were animus against the book, though not quite enough for it to be punished by the Library Committee with public destruction or burning. No reverence, obviously, was thought to be due to the legacy of a former fellow, but the book passed on to the hands of the fellow of another college, for it was inscribed in what one could only call a precise, lilliputian and almost pedantic hand, with his name and the date September, '88. As it was the name of a man still alive, several years younger than I, the author of books that even I, with my high tolerance for the arcane and pedantic, have no intention of reading, I cannot give his name here. But there still remains the mystery of the book's final appearance on the shelves of Oxfam in Bridgnorth.

Frederic Hillersdon Keeling was born in 1886, attended Winchester and Cambridge, and was killed during the First World War on 18 August 1916. He was leading an audacious grenade attack when he was shot, dying instantly. He left behind him this volume of letters (how many he wrote, and at what length!), and one book, *Child Labour in the United Kingdom – A Study of the Development and Administration of the Law Relating to the Employment of Children*: an important subject, no doubt, but not a title to set the heart racing.

Keeling was a political radical from an early age, impelled (so H.G. Wells suggests) by the bourgeois complacency of his parents and the peaceful suburban banality of his home life. His letters are certainly not without interest or even wider significance, for they illuminate the mental life of a certain important class of person early in the twentieth century, privileged but restless and dissatisfied, perhaps guilty at its own good fortune. The letters are at once egotistical and concerned with the life about him. Thanks to his attendance at Cambridge, he soon mingled with the first men of his time, at least the first men in reformist circles, such as Bernard Shaw, Beatrice and Sidney Webb (Beatrice being an honorary man), H.G. Wells, Ramsay Macdonald (who was to become the first Labour Prime Minister), and Hugh Dalton (who was to be Chancellor of the Exchequer under Clement Atlee).

Keeling was certainly no hypocrite: he never sought, or obtained, lucrative employment, and for several years worked in Leeds for the Labour Exchange to obtain a thorough knowledge of industrial conditions, engage on research and provide practical advice for men of the working class. He attended innumerable socialist meetings and wrote articles for obscure local socialist publications. Being nevertheless a member of the privileged classes, he managed to travel widely and wrote articles for the *New Statesman* about, for example, the independence of Albania. If he wanted time in the countryside, he always knew someone with a delightful house or cottage to lend him. It is always easier to see the misfortunes of others than one's own good fortune.

There is much to be learnt from this book, though not surprisingly there is a considerable quantity of *whither am I going?* type of young man's reflection to wade through in order to obtain it. One learns, for example, that so-called *Cancel culture* is really nothing new, though it has undergone a gestalt switch as to who should be cancelled. When Keeling was at Cambridge, socialists were a very tiny and despised minority, and rowdies tried to break up their meetings. To allow others to speak their mind is not a basic human instinct.

Very early, Keeling developed an antagonism to the family as an institution or form of social arrangement. He said that he was a collectivist, and his early ambition was to be a member of the administrative class of philanthropical bureaucrats who would replace capitalists in the interests of all. The family was an obstacle to this vision, as well as to individual self-fulfilment. Keeling was not alone in this, for he wrote:

> If we are ever to break the family or — which is a better way of putting it — secure liberty for other forms of social organization, it will be, not primarily through the dissemination of theories, but because of growth of personal dislike of the institution, which I find a very large proportion of my friends have in common with me. It is one of my dreams that through my numerous and growing friendships with Cambridge and Oxford and other Socialists of my generation I may be able to do something to create a large enough body of opinion to make a development in those other forms which are to supersede family organizations possible.

Si monumentum requiris circumspice.

Nevertheless, Keeling married early and quickly had two children, though he never lived with his wife and was only very marginally involved with his children's upbringing. When he went to war, he was very pleased to have fathered — his word for it — two children, but he seemed to be pleased mainly on biological grounds.

While working in Leeds, he became a little disillusioned by the wonders to be wrought by an enlightened bureaucracy, even one created for beneficent ends. While 'my religion, my whole philosophy of the business of life, centres round the State,' his dream of being part of 'a new model army supplanting property by organization inch by inch,' yet he discovered a little later that 'What I have seen with regard to the nature and growth of official machinery gives me furiously to think.' What he saw was official stupidity and self-interest. This surprised him, and later he ceased to be a socialist or believe in any magical solutions to the evils he still saw around him. But he had named his son Bernard Sidney, after Shaw and Webb, in his opinion the two greatest men of the age.

There are other interesting things tucked away in this book. When, in 1911, he went to Germany, he discussed German colonial policy in South West Africa, where he gave as his opinion that British colonial policy was better than German. It was more commercially sound to educate and civilise than to exterminate, as the Germans were doing quite openly, according to their own officials. He expressed no particular outrage at this, however.

Some of his letters were addressed to R.C.K. Ensor, which no doubt explains the latter's donation of the book to Corpus

Christi College's library.

When he was killed, Keeling's commanding officer was R. Barrington-Ward, later editor of the *Times*. Barrington-Ward died of malaria in 1948, on his way back to England from a trip to Uganda, and was buried in Dar-es-Salaam.

In his last letter, written four days before he was killed, Keeling wrote:

> What a blessed and comforting doctrine the idea of fate is! It does somehow enter into the soul of a soldier. I see no one around worrying about going into battle.

I bought a book by accident, or rather by mistake. I was preparing a chapter for a projected work about the unread writers buried in Highgate Cemetery in London, similar to one that I had written about Père-Lachaise in Paris. Among these authors was Sir Leslie Stephen. Perhaps Stephen is not quite forgotten historically — he was, after all, the father of Virginia Woolf and the founding editor of the *Dictionary of National Biography* — but I think that no one reads him now.

Anyhow, the book I bought by mistake was a book that I thought was by him. It was by Sir *Somebody* Stephen, and the wish being father to the perception, I assumed it was by Sir Leslie Stephen, though in fact it was by his brother, who had also been knighted, Sir James Fitzjames Stephen, the legal scholar and political philosopher. This book, *Horae Sabbaticae*, was published in 1892, at which date Leslie had not yet been knighted, but my enthusiasm got the better of me, and I persisted in reading *Sir James* as *Sir Leslie*. As Karl Popper said, hypothesis always precedes perception.

The book had on its front pastedown the bookplate of James Howard Helm, whom I have been unable, after perfunctory efforts, to trace. The bookplate shows a monk sitting on the ground with a large folio volume resting on his knee. The motto above him is in French: *Un livre est un ami qui ne change jamais* — A book is a friend who never changes — which causes one to speculate on James Howard Helm's experience of humanity.

But is it true that books do not change? They change physically, as do humans: their pages yellow or are foxed, their spines crack, their edges become rubbed. Perhaps they do not die in quite the same way as humans do, but certainly they can be, and have been, cremated. They go into retirement and work no more. It is not for nothing that we say of a man who has lost his former position or status that he is now on the shelf.

As to change and friendship, interesting questions arise. We change not only physically but mentally with age: and if friends' ideas — or tastes — grow apart, do they remain friends? It depends — but on what? The extent of the difference, the depth of the friendship in the first place? It is a common experience that a book that seemed marvellous, revelatory, profound at one time in a life may appear none of those things at a later age, and a person may be genuinely bemused by what he ever saw in it. He may even be appalled by the confrontation with the superficiality or bad taste of his former self. Is it true, then, that a book is a friend that never changes? Our interpretation of a text, fixed physically in print, may certainly change. Is the change in us, or in the book? We outgrow books as we may outgrow friends.

Sir James Fitzjames Stephen, Leslie Stephen's brother and Virginia Woolf's uncle, is now remembered, if he is remembered at all, first as the author of a long demolition of John Stuart Mill's eloquent tract, *On Liberty*, but perhaps more as the judge in the trial of Florence Maybrick, who was accused of having poisoned her husband to death with arsenic dissolved from fly-papers, and who was convicted, sentenced to death, reprieved and eventually pardoned. Stephen was severely criticised for his conduct of the trial, in which he was said to have exhibited gross partiality in favour of the prosecution. Certainly, Mrs Maybrick's barrister, Sir Charles Russell, fought for years on her behalf, eventually succeeding. She returned to her native America, where she died in poverty and obscurity in 1940.

At the time of her trial, in 1890, Sir James Fitzjames Stephen's intellectual powers were in steep decline, and he was soon afterwards persuaded to step down from the bench.

Horae Sabbaticae (of which mine was the third in the series) is a collection of articles contributed by Stephen to the *Saturday Review* — or to give it its full title, *The Saturday Review of Politics, Literature, Science and Arts*, which ran from the 1850s to the 1930s — its slow decline lasting decades, like that of the country in which it was published. (No one nowadays would try to sell a publication with such a title.) But in its heyday, it published Anthony Trollope, Walter Bagehot, and Oscar Wilde, apart from Stephen.

His contributions were mainly philosophical or political in a broad sense. It is possible to follow James Howard Helm's interests by the pages in the book that he bothered to cut —

the rest remained uncut until I bought the book more than a hundred and thirty years after it was published. Mr Helm was interested in Edmund Burke, Alexis de Tocqueville, and Joseph de Maistre, but not in Bishop Berkeley, William Paley or Jeremy Bentham. He read the essay on the works of Burke on 21 March, 1904, according to a pencil mark, but *The Rights of Conscience* (by which Stephen meant the freedom of moral judgment) did not interest him.

In this essay, Stephen tackles a very large subject indeed, within the compass of eighteen not very closely printed pages. If he does not resolve in that short compass the problems and dilemmas that he raises, one can hardly blame him, for thousands of books and millions of words have been written without any universally accepted solution having been found.

There is, for example, the question of whether moral standards are relative or absolute — or perhaps both, as light is both particle and wave. Here, in a few lines, is summarised the difference between relativists and absolutists:

> A great deal has been said... on the difference between the moral judgments of different times and countries, and of different individuals of the same time and country. It has been asserted with some vehemence, on the one side, that the virtues of one age are the vices of another; and it has been said with equal warmth, on the other side, that no nation ever approved of ingratitude, or cruelty, or perfidy as such, although under particular circumstances they may have applauded actions which others would have [condemned utterly].

Stephen says that 'The Englishman of a hundred years ago thought it not cruel to hang people for horse-stealing[52] or to bait bulls, or set cocks to fight. Many Englishmen now think it cruel to hang men for murder.' And yet, at the same time, 'Ancient Greeks and Englishmen of the eighteenth century have all agreed in the general conclusion that there are cases in which the causing of pain was wrong, and that the disposition to cause pain in such cases was common enough to require distinct dyslogistic [disapproving] epithet.'

We are all agreed that cruelty is wrong, but not as to what constitutes cruelty. Sometimes, we have to be cruel to be kind, though Nietzsche would more likely say that we are always kind to be cruel.

I understand the arguments for relativism, which are strong: it is just that I am convinced that my own judgments, at least for the time being, are absolute.

To my great surprise, I have again reached the end of my notebook, and, as on the three previous occasions, I will pay tribute to the involuntary furnisher of my title, Dylan Thomas.

Whenever I think of him, I think of the concept of natural or congenital genius, of which he seems to me a clear example. And then, by association of ideas, I think back to a scene in, of all places, Guatemala. I was driving round the country in

---

[52] 'Sir,' said an English judge to a man whom he was sentencing to death for horse-stealing, 'you are not to be hanged for stealing a horse, but that horses may not be stolen.' On this theory, any punishment is justified if it deters.

the white pickup truck that I had bought there for what seems to me the enormous price of $2000. I was in the habit of picking up anyone by the side of the road who asked for a lift, and I think I will be allowed out of hell one day every ten thousand years because of the prayers of some humble peasants for whom I had stopped.

When they alighted at their destination, or the nearest to their destination that the road took them, the elder of the group came to the cabin of the truck and with a humility that made me feel guilty at my unmerited good fortune asked me how much they owed me.

'*Nada*,' I said — nothing.

'*Que Dios le bendiga*,' he said — May God bless you.

I was moved by the peasants' honesty, and by the humble man's dignity. I had refused payment that he might think that not everyone was a grasping swine out to exploit such as they, which was an impression easy enough to receive in the Guatemala of the time.

I also picked up an American hitch-hiker a few years younger than I. He was a student and a Marxist. I cannot recall how or why the subject came up, but we fell to talking about the idea of inborn genius. He thought the notion of genius almost fascist because it was a denial of the equality of Man, not in its ethical, but in its substantive, empirical sense. Because he wanted to deny the influence of heredity altogether on human capabilities, he felt obliged to deny any difference that was not the pure product of environmental influence.

'Still,' I said, as we drove past fields of maize, 'there is only one Mozart.'

For him, however, Mozart was only the inevitable product of a concatenation of environmental influences. Mozart could have been anybody.

Now it seems to me that Dylan Thomas, albeit at a lower level, was also a born genius. I have read the letters between him and Vernon Watkins, another poet of South-West Wales, who was his friend from adolescence. Watkins was an intelligent and cultivated man, more highly-educated than Thomas, but the letters between them demonstrate clearly that Thomas's verbal inventiveness was far greater than that of Watkins, and extraordinary from the first. No doubt Thomas's rackety life in part explains the far greater interest in him than in Watkins, but there is a great difference in the level of their poetic accomplishment.

I stayed twice in South-West Wales, first in Carmarthen and then in Llanelli. I regularly visited the second-hand bookshop in Swansea, owned by Jeff Towns, a serious scholar of Dylan Thomas's life and work. It was he who introduced me to the work of an unjustly neglected Welsh author, Rhys Davies, and he who invited me to his public interview in Swansea of Gwen Watkins, the widow of Thomas's friend, Vernon Watkins: a remarkable woman in her own right, having played a part in the decrypting of the German military code during the war. (She died, aged 101, two weeks before I wrote this.) It was obvious from the interview that she didn't much care for Thomas, and I suspected, or surmised, albeit without any positive evidence, that it was in part because he so overshadowed her husband in public esteem, while at the same time being far the worse-behaved man. It hadn't occurred to me that someone might not be susceptible to

Thomas's charm or unforgiving of his obvious sins and tendency to exploit people simply because he was an evident genius.

Thomas's linguistic felicity could not have been taught. His book of autobiographical short stories, *Portrait of the Artist as a Young Dog*, was published when he was 26, by which time he had written many of his greatest poems. His writing was already distinctive and, to me, full of delight. Here is the first sentence of a story, *Old Garbo*:

> Mr Parr trod delicately and disgustedly down the dark, narrow stairs like a man on mice.

What a brilliant image, a man treading on mice! I could never have written such a thing. Thomas manages it over and over, the brilliance emerging from his pen in a seemingly unstoppable flow — though in fact he worked hard and revised often. (I am reminded of Mozart's letter to Haydn when he sent the six quartets that he dedicated to him. He has studied hard and laboured over them, he said, so that they should sound spontaneous.)

The stories in *Portrait of the Artist* are amusing but also moving. Can a truly egocentric person enter so successfully into the feelings of others, such as to cause us to sympathise with them?

Thomas had the gift, as had Dickens, of seeing the world through the eyes of a child, or of the child that he was. The story, *Patricia, Edith and Arnold*, illustrates this ability. Patricia is the servant of Thomas's parents, while Edith is the servant next door. They both receive love letters from Arnold, a young man, written in exactly the same words, with precisely the same terms of endearment. One day, after Patricia and Edith have discovered this, they are walking with the young Dylan in the park when they meet Arnold and demand to know which of them he really loves. He tries to say that he loves both of them, but they force him to choose. He chooses Patricia, who then berates him for having deceived her friend, Edith. It is all related beautifully though the semi-comprehending eyes of the child.

In *Who Do You Wish Was with Us*, Thomas recounts a visit to the beach (poetically described) with his friend, Roy, on a bank holiday. Roy's father and brother have died, and his mother is in a wheelchair. Here is a searing passage that reminds us of the world that, all to the good, we have almost lost:

'I've never seen such a lot of gulls,' I said. 'Have you ever seen such a lot? Such a lot of gulls. You try and count them. Two of them are fighting up there; look, pecking each other like hens in the air. What'll you bet that the big one wins? Old dirty beak! I wouldn't like to have had his dinner, a bit of sheep and dead gulls.' I swore at myself for saying the word "dead". 'Wasn't it gay in town this morning?'

Roy stared at his hand. Nothing could stop him now. 'Wasn't it gay in town this morning? Everyone laughing and smiling in their summer outfits. The kids were playing and everybody was happy; they almost had the band out[53]. I used to hold my father down when he had fits. I had to change the sheets twice a day for my brother, there was blood on everything. I watched him getting thinner and thinner; in the end you could lift him up with one hand.[54] And his wife wouldn't go to see him because he coughed in her face. Mother couldn't move, and I had to cook as well, cook and nurse and change the sheets and hold father down when he got mad.'

I say that we have almost lost this world, but I too have known families or individuals who have attracted a disproportionate share of misfortune. The world is worse than unjust — it is unfair.

---

[53] In those days, brass bands would play on promenades.
[54] Clearly, he had tuberculosis, common in Wales at the time, and still incurable.